ESCAPE

Children of the
Holocaust

===

Allan Zullo

SCHOLASTIC INC.
New York Toronto London Auckland Sydney
Mexico City New Delhi Hong Kong Buenos Aires

To all the children of the Holocaust
who escaped from the clutches of the Nazis
and their collaborators

ISBN-13: 978-0-545-09929-5
ISBN-10: 0-545-09929-3

Copyright © 2009 by The Wordsellers, Inc.

12 11 10 9 8 7 6 5 4 3 2 1   10 11 12 13 14/0

Printed in the U.S.A.
First Scholastic printing, September 2009

Acknowledgments

I wish to extend my heartfelt gratitude to the Holocaust survivors featured in this book for their willingness to relive, in personal interviews with me, their painful and emotional memories of the horrors they experienced as children before, during, and after their escapes from death.

I also want to thank the following for their much-appreciated cooperation and guidance: Ronnie Jacobs Cohen, Director, Community Relations Council and Holocaust Programs, United Jewish Federation of Tidewater, Virginia Beach, Virginia (**www.Jewishva.org**); Anne Grenn Saldinger, Ph.D., Director, Oral History Project, Holocaust Center of Northern California, San Francisco, California (**www.hcnc.org**); Survivor Affairs, United States Holocaust Memorial Museum, Washington, D.C. (**www. ushmm.org/remembrance/survivoraffairs**); and Deborah Miles, Executive Director, Center for Diversity Education, Asheville, North Carolina (**www.diversityed.org**).

Author's Note

You are about to read seven incredible true stories of brave boys and girls who escaped from the clutches of the Nazis during the Holocaust. These accounts are based exclusively on the personal, lengthy interviews I conducted with each survivor featured in this book. Using real names, dates, and places, these stories are factual versions of the survivors' recollections. However, the dialogue has been re-created for dramatic effect. (The words *Nazis* and *Germans* are used interchangeably.)

Much of what you will read in the following pages is disturbing because that's the way it really happened. It's hard to imagine that anyone, especially children, could bear such cruelty.

But this book is also a celebration of the human spirit — of the will to overcome unspeakable horrors, the will to triumph over evil, the will to live. Each person's experience reveals that in the most hopeless situations, people can rely on their courage, faith, and smarts — and sometimes sheer luck — to escape from almost certain death.

Not only did these brave young people survive the Holocaust, but also they grew up, got married, and have enjoyed happy, productive lives. All of them, too, have turned their harrowing experiences into lessons for future generations by speaking at schools, churches, synagogues, conferences, and other gatherings.

I hope you find the extraordinary stories in this book inspiring, and that you understand how important it is to keep recalling the past . . . so no one ever forgets.

—Allan Zullo

Contents

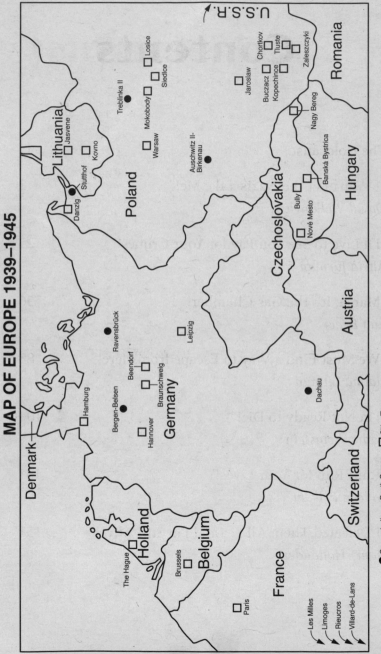

MAP OF EUROPE 1939–1945

U.S.S.R.

Romania

Losice
Chortkov
Tluste
Siedlce
Zaleszczyki
Jaroslaw
Treblinka II
Buczacz
Kopechince
Mokobody
Nagy Bereg
Lithuania
Jasvene
Kovno
Warsaw
Banská Bystrica
Stutthof
Poland
Auschwitz II-Birkenau
Hungary
Danzig
Bully
Czechoslovakia
Nové Mesto
Ravensbrück
Leipzig
Austria
Beendorf
Braunschweig
Bergen-Belsen
Germany
Dachau
Hamburg
Hannover
Switzerland
The Hague
Holland
Belgium
Brussels
France
Paris
Les Milles
Limoges
Rieucros
Villard-de-Lans
Denmark

● Concentration or Death Camps   □ Cities/Towns

The Holocaust

Led by dictator Adolf Hitler, the Nazi Party in Germany in the 1930s and 1940s believed that certain people—especially Jews, Gypsies, and the disabled—were inferior and didn't deserve to live.

The Nazis were anti-Semitic, which means they hated the Jewish people. Although many Jews were doctors, lawyers, business people, bankers, and teachers who contributed a great deal to German society, Hitler blamed them for the country's economic problems. The truth was that Germany was going through a difficult time because it was badly defeated in World War I, which ended in 1918.

Hitler and his parliament passed laws that required Jews to give up their jobs, homes, businesses, and rights. To enforce these laws, the police organization known as the Gestapo and an elite army corps known as the S.S. imprisoned, beat, and murdered Jews—simply because they were Jewish. Many Jews and political enemies of the Nazis were sent to brutal prisons known as concentration camps.

Hitler was determined to protect at all costs "German blood and German honor" for the country's Aryans, the name given to white, non-Jewish Germans. He also was determined to invade and occupy all of Europe.

In March 1938, Germany annexed Austria (which a majority of non-Jewish Austrians welcomed) and put into effect harsh new laws stripping Jews of their rights. Next, Germany annexed parts of Czechoslovakia and influenced pro-Nazi governments in Hungary and Slovakia to establish anti-Jewish laws.

Then in September 1939, Poland was invaded, triggering World War II. Because of a secret prewar agreement, Germany occupied the western half of the country while the Soviet Union (including Russia) controlled the eastern half.

Great Britain and France, who were allies of Poland, declared war on Germany. The following year, Nazi forces invaded and occupied Denmark, Norway, Belgium, Holland, and Luxembourg. Then France fell, and Great Britain was battered by German air assaults. Next, Germany launched a surprise attack against Russia in June 1941 and occupied such Soviet countries as Lithuania and the Ukraine. In December 1941, the United States entered the war and joined Great Britain and the Free French (an organization fighting for the liberation of France) to form the Allied Powers, which were determined to halt the German war machine. The Soviet Union joined the Allies, too.

Also fighting the Nazis in German-occupied territory were secret groups of brave citizens known as the underground, the Resistance, and partisans. These rebels for freedom (some of them Jews) used hit-and-run guerilla

tactics and sabotage against the German army and h[
Jews escape.

As country after country fell under German occupation, Jews were singled out for mistreatment, just as they were in Germany. They had to wear the six-pointed Star of David, a symbol of Judaism, on their sleeves, chests, or backs to set them apart from non-Jews. They couldn't walk freely in the streets or do many of the things other Europeans took for granted. Signs in theaters, cafés, restaurants, and other public places warned that Jews weren't allowed to enter.

During the war years, the Nazis created ghettos. These were small areas inside cities that were sealed up by brick or stone walls or barbed wire, where Jews were forced to live under unhealthy and crowded conditions. Every month, tens of thousands of Jews were deported—moved to forced-labor camps or concentration camps where, unless they were useful to the Nazis, they were killed in gas chambers or murdered in some other way. It was all part of Hitler's Final Solution, the Nazi plan to eliminate all the Jews of Europe.

Why would such cruelty go virtually unchecked? Out of fear, anti-Semitism, or self-protection, millions of non-Jewish Europeans couldn't or wouldn't get involved in stopping the Nazi madness. It's estimated that only one half of one percent of European non-Jews—some of them known as Righteous Gentiles—risked their lives to assist and hide Jews from the Nazis. Sadly, many Europeans actively supported the Nazis by turning in Jews and those who assisted Jews. These morally bankrupt people were known as collaborators, informants, or Nazi sympathizers.

As the war came to an end in 1945, the Allies liberated the remaining imprisoned or hidden Jews, although hundreds of thousands were barely alive because of Nazi cruelty. The world was shocked to discover that of the nine million Jews who lived in Europe before the war, six million (including three million Polish Jews) had been murdered or died from starvation or disease in Nazi camps. Of the Jewish children who failed to escape from Europe after 1939, more than 1.5 million were murdered by the Nazis or were deported to camps where they died of illness or hunger. Another four million non-Jewish civilians died at the hands of the Nazis.

This horrific mass murder is called the Holocaust, a word from ancient Greece meaning "sacrifice by fire." Over time, the word came to mean the deliberate and systematic slaughter of a large number of human beings.

Out of the ashes of the Holocaust emerged Israel—the rebirth of the Jewish homeland—where in 1948 hundreds of thousands of Jews started a new life free from the tyranny of hate. Many other Holocaust survivors chose to remain in Europe, come to America, or settle in other continents, hoping to put together the pieces of their shattered lives. They each had a story to tell, but over the decades, the world still has heard too few of them. Now, with each passing year, the number of Holocaust survivors dwindles as they pass on from old age.

Their stories deserve to be told before it is too late.

"I Won't Let the Nazis Take Me!"

≡

David Wolkowitz

As David Wolkowitz dressed for breakfast in his dormitory at the orphanage, he heard a strange rumble in the distance. Glancing out the window, he saw a billowing dust cloud advancing along the country road. David began feeling jittery. *What is it?* he wondered. The noise grew into loud throbbing sounds that resonated off the hilly French landscape. The ominous din came closer. *Oh, please don't be what I think it is.* The morning sun finally revealed the source of the racket: motorcycles and army trucks. David gasped and yelled, "The Nazis are coming!"

At lunch in the dining hall the day before, the director of the orphanage had made an announcement that stunned the 100 Jewish boys who had been living there for the past 18 months, waiting out the war: "The mayor and the police chief have informed me of a report that the Nazis might carry out a raid on the orphanage sometime in the near future and take away everyone who is sixteen and older. We must stay on the alert."

When David heard the news, he turned to his friend Samuel and moaned, "They said we would be safe here, that the Nazis would leave us alone."

Seeing the color drain from David's face, Samuel said, "I know it's bad for the older boys, but we won't have to worry. The Nazis won't take us because we're only thirteen."

"But I *look* sixteen," David claimed. "I'm tall for my age and I have no papers, no proof of my real age. What's to stop them from taking me away with the others?"

"I never thought of that. I don't have any proof, either."

So when David saw the German army vehicles roaring toward the orphanage that summer morning in 1943, he knew exactly what he was going to do. "I won't let the Nazis take me! I'm leaving right now!"

"So am I," Samuel said.

The other boys in the dorm at the time were much younger and didn't have the same reason to fear the enemy, so they made no attempt to run off.

David and Samuel climbed out of a second-floor window and scrambled down the vines that covered the wall. Just as they landed on the ground, a horse-drawn wagon carrying garbage rattled past the orphanage. "Follow me," David urged his buddy. They hopped on the back and made their getaway.

After a few miles, they jumped off and ran into the woods. "We should go our separate ways," David said. "Two Jewish boys wandering the countryside together will attract suspicion." Samuel agreed. They shook hands and wished each other luck.

Watching Samuel disappear into the forest, David felt his body tremble with misgivings. Running his shaking fingers through his curly dark hair, he took stock of his situation: *I'm all alone. I have no money and only the clothes on my back. The countryside is crawling with Nazis who would kill me and collaborators who would turn me in. I'm scared to death. What do I do?*

To calm himself, he summoned warm images of his early childhood in Leipzig, Germany, the music capital of Europe and home to famous composers such as Bach, Mendelssohn, and Wagner. David grew up surrounded by music. His father, Abraham—the boy called him Pappi—was a conductor, arranger, composer, and superb musician. His mother, Regina—whom David called Mutti—was a concert pianist and music teacher.

Leaning against a tree, David imagined hearing the music of his childhood.

Musicians come to the Wolkowitzes' large apartment for their weekly get-together with his parents and play chamber music. It's after David's bedtime, so he quietly sneaks out of bed and opens the door so he can hear them better.

Now David is seven, and he's watching in fascina-tion as his father conducts the orchestra in Leipzig. David is wearing a black velvet suit with short pants, frilly white shirt, and knee-high white socks with tas-sels hanging from their tops. Abraham hands him the baton, which is almost as big as the boy is, and David proudly conducts the orchestra.

Stop daydreaming, David scolded himself. *That was a lifetime ago. I need to concentrate on finding a way to survive.* He had assumed he would remain in the orphanage until the end of the war, but here he was, miles away, having just fled from the Nazi raid. Mustering his courage, he decided, *I'll walk to Switzerland. It's a neutral country, so I'll be safe there.* He wasn't sure how far it was, but he knew to head east toward the Alps. He had a few things in his favor: He was fit, resourceful, and could speak French.

Off he marched. Occasionally, he would stop at a farm-house and tell a made-up story of how he was a poor French boy who had been separated from his parents during the chaos of war, was trying to make his way back home, and could the good farmer please spare some bread and cheese? Sometimes his plea worked; sometimes it didn't.

More than once, a farmer's wife fed him, but her husband became suspicious and left to get the authori-ties. David always managed to leave before he was confronted. He never knew whom he could really trust, so he relied on gut instinct. Trekking from one village to the next, he stayed focused on his goal—reaching Switzerland.

Throughout the days, mental pictures of his family never strayed far from his thoughts.

After attending services at the synagogue with his father on Friday nights, David, an only child, celebrates Shabbat (the Sabbath) at home with his parents and maternal grandparents, Herman and Salomea Jedlitzki, who live with the family. His grandmother, whom he calls Oma, lights the Sabbath candles, and his grandfather, whom he calls Opa, chants the kiddush (blessing of the Sabbath). For Shabbat dinner, they eat cold boiled carp, chicken soup, and roast chicken.

But his memories began to darken after 1935 when Germany passed laws that stripped all Jews of their civil rights, and anti-Semitism spread like a cancer, afflicting victims of all ages.

While walking to their Jewish school—Jews are no longer allowed to attend public schools—David and his cousin Wolfgang encounter non-Jewish children who taunt them, hurl stones at them, and strike them with sticks.

"Mutti, why do they call me a dirty Jew?" six-year-old David asks. "I took a bath."

Months of walking dragged on for David. To stave off hunger, he picked fruit off trees and stole food from gardens and farms. He also ate in soup kitchens set up by churches to feed the countless number of displaced people who were roaming the battle-scarred countryside.

Sometimes David caught a short ride on the back of a farmer's hay wagon, but mostly he walked. He'd catch a little sleep in barns, on park benches, or in the forest. He had no change of clothes, so whenever he reached a stream, he bathed and washed his garb. His shoes were falling apart, so he wrapped them with string and stuffed the holes in his soles with rags.

He tried to stay positive, as best as a lonely 13-year-old could in his dire situation. But there were times he felt angry. It didn't have to be this way.

Believing it's best to leave Germany, David's parents, Abraham and Regina, make arrangements for the three of them to immigrate to the United States. His grand-parents insist on staying. In 1937, the Wolkowitzes travel to The Hague, Holland, with just a few belong-ings, including his father's favorite violin. The Nazis don't allow the Jews to take anything of value out of the country, but they let Abraham keep his precious instrument. While waiting in The Hague for their final immigration papers, Regina can't bring herself to leave her parents, so she, Abraham, and David return to Leipzig.

Back home, the Nazis refuse to let Abraham resume his job as an orchestra conductor. He can find work only as a shoe repairman. It pains young David to see his father — an accomplished musician with such delicate hands — come home every night with fingers so bloodied he can't play his beloved instruments.

On his trek toward Switzerland, David was always on edge. Whenever he saw a German patrol or Nazi-sympathizing French police approaching in the distance — a daily occurrence — he hid in the woods or behind a building. Nights were always the worst because they spawned such bad memories.

October 1938. Two Gestapo agents, backed by several armed S.S. officers with drawn guns, storm into the apartment and tell David's grandparents, "You have one hour to pack one suitcase each."

"But where are we going?" Opa asks.

"We're taking you to the train station. You're being deported to Poland."

His grandparents, who were born in Poland, had lived in Germany for nearly 30 years but had retained their Polish citizenship, so there is nothing they can do. No amount of pleading and crying can sway the Gestapo into granting them more time.

Confused and scared, David clutches his grandparents and cries out, "Oma! Opa! Don't go!" The

S.S. officers pry them from his arms and hustle them away.

Now it's November 9, 1938 — forever known as Kristallnacht (the Night of Broken Glass). Roving gangs of Nazis trash and loot the stores of Jewish merchants, burn down synagogues, and brutally beat and, in some cases, kill Jews.

From the second-floor window of their apartment, David watches in stark terror the mayhem outside and sees the sky turning red from the fires. His mother pulls him away from the window because she doesn't want the Gestapo to see them. Still, David hears screams in the streets as Jews coming home from work are attacked. At least his parents are home to offer him comfort.

As David approached the square in a small village near the city of Clermont-Ferrand, he noticed a young boy about his age leaning against a stone wall, playing French folk tunes on a flute. David, who hadn't heard such beautiful music in a long time, went up to him and said, "I admire your playing."

"Thank you. I'd go crazy without my music. It makes me forget about this ugly war."

David and the boy, whose name was Joel, hung out together for three days. But over the following two days, David couldn't find him. *It's time to move on, anyway.* As he headed out of town, David spotted Joel leaning against the same stone wall, but this time his flute was silent.

Then David saw why. Both of Joel's hands were heavily bandaged.

"Joel, what happened?"

Joel stared glumly at his hands and replied, "A couple of days ago, I saw a metal thing lying in the grass and I picked it up. I was examining it when it exploded and blew off fingers on both hands."

"I'm so sorry for you."

Joel spat and said, "I hate that I won't ever play my flute again. I hate this war."

I have to get to Switzerland, David thought. And so he kept walking. Fall gave way to winter. His hat and light jacket were no match for the brutally cold winds that swept down the French Alps. Still, he continued his trek up the mountains toward what he believed would be his safe haven.

Of course, he once thought Brussels, Belgium, would be a safe haven, too. That's where he and his parents had fled to start a new life in early 1939 after his grandparents had been deported. Abraham and Regina resumed their music careers, and the boy went to public school, where he learned to speak French and Flemish fluently.

In the family's two-room Brussels apartment, David reads letters from Oma and Opa, who are living in the Jewish ghetto in Warsaw, Poland. But it's hard for him to know what's really happening to them because censors in German-occupied Poland have blacked out half the lines in the letters.

Mail also arrives from David's aunt and uncle, Golda (Regina's sister) and Leo Katz and their children, who had lived one block from the Wolkowitzes in Leipzig before the war. They write about life in their new home in the United States, where they had immigrated after fleeing Germany. David stares at the return address of every envelope the Katzes send and wishes that one day he, too, could live at 316 Commonwealth Avenue, Buffalo, New York, USA.

The higher David climbed in the Alps, the lower the temperatures dropped. *I need to get across the mountains before I freeze to death*, he told himself. *I'm so close.* But as he neared the Swiss border, he heard spurts of gunfire. He scrambled to a vantage point and felt his heart sink. The Germans had set up a machine-gun nest at the mountain pass David had planned to cross. He tried a different route that skirted the enemy, but when he reached the next pass, he discovered that it, too, was patrolled by the German soldiers. *I can practically see Switzerland. I can't give up now.*

David felt desperate. He hadn't eaten in a couple of days, and his body ached from the frigid conditions. He was starting to feel panicky. He soon met a small group of refugees who were carrying bundles on their backs. "You can't get into Switzerland," the leader told David. "The Germans have set up machine-gun nests at every mountain pass. They're picking off people foolish enough to try to reach the border."

David was crushed. *All that walking, all that begging for food and stealing from gardens . . . for what?* He was tired and cold and hungry, so the dejected boy turned around and hiked down the mountain with no goal other than to survive. He felt just as anxious and lost as he did in the days following May 10, 1940.

David is awakened by wailing sirens, explosions, and gunfire. Germany is attacking Belgium, which doesn't have an army strong enough to repel the rapidly advancing invaders.

Knowing they won't be safe anymore in Belgium, Abraham and Regina decide they and David will escape to neighboring France. But because they don't have passports or the proper papers, they must try to sneak in illegally. Abraham, taking his prized violin with him, leaves first and plans to contact them once he enters France.

Days go by without word from him, and David and his mother can wait no longer. They leave Brussels on the train for France—a country now partly occupied by Germany. The train carries mostly women and children. Wherever he looks, David sees death and destruction, chaos and confusion. Tens of thousands are fleeing in cars, in horse-drawn wagons, and on foot.

For more than ten days, the train crisscrosses northern France in a frantic journey to nowhere. It stops and starts, is shuffled from track to track, and chugs in one direction and then another in a desperate effort to avoid getting strafed, bombed, shelled, or caught in the crossfire between French and German troops.

Look out! *David ducks for cover under the seat when German planes swoop down and pepper the train with bullets.*

What's that whistling sound? Bombs are dropping! *Just as the train pulls out of the station of the French town of Dieppe, German bombs rain down and destroy the station.*

Finally, the train stops for good in a small town in northern France, where everyone is ordered off. When David and his mother can't produce any valid papers, they are arrested and sent to a crude prison in a farm compound, where they sleep on a bale of hay in a horse stable. Two weeks later, they are taken by train to the Rieucros internment camp in southern France, where hundreds of women and children are kept under armed guard in ramshackle wooden barracks surrounded by barbed wire.

After turning around from the Swiss border, David walked aimlessly throughout southeastern France. He entered the cities of Lyon and Grenoble, but because they were teeming with German soldiers, he left for safer smaller towns. *I can't keep walking forever,* he told himself. *Who knows how long this war will last?*

Hearing about a Catholic priest who was sympathetic to the plight of the Jews, David hiked to the mountain village of Villard-de-Lans. He found the priest and told him his story. The priest, known as Monsieur le Curé, immediately sent a housekeeper to bring David fresh clothes and shoes to replace his tattered garments and footwear. That evening, the young teenager had his first hot meal in months and slept in a comfortable bed in the priest's residence. The two formed a quick bond, partly because the priest shared David's love for classical music and had a large record library.

David and Monsieur le Curé agreed to tell everyone that the boy was a Catholic orphaned by the war. That fib required David to attend Mass every Sunday and follow the rituals and traditions of the Church, which he tried to do — up to a point.

"Monsieur le Curé," David told him, "I am grateful to be here. But I'm Jewish, and my faith doesn't allow me to kneel during prayer the way Catholics do during Mass."

The priest nodded. "I understand. From now on, when the rest of us kneel during Mass, just lean forward in the pew to give the appearance that you're kneeling. That way you can stay true to your religion and not raise any suspicions that you're not Catholic."

"Thank you. I'll do that."

Monsieur le Curé put his hand on the boy's shoulder and said, "The Nazis have taken away your parents and all your possessions. But remember, David, the one thing they will never be able to take away from you is your Jewish heritage."

Like all the prisoners at Rieucros, mother and son sleep on wooden shelves with only a straw mattress and rough horsehair blanket for bedding. Night after night, David wakes up screaming as rats scamper over his body.

Breakfast consists of a piece of dark, hard bread and coffee made from roasted roots. Lunch and dinner are the same—a bowl of soup, which is nothing more than hot water with a few pieces of cabbage leaves or rutabaga. The food is barely enough to keep them alive. Because of horrible sanitary conditions and vermin infestation, the muddy and stinky camp becomes a breeding ground for disease. David and Regina are always sick, usually with dysentery. He is getting alarmed that his mother, once a blonde beauty, is growing old, gaunt, and pale with worry about their future—or if they even have one.

For weeks, David and Regina have no clue about Abraham's fate. Then one day they are notified that he had been arrested while trying to enter France and is now toiling in the notoriously awful Gurs labor camp in the Pyrenees, the mountain range that separates France from Spain.

But their spirits soar when, with the help of friends and relatives in the United States, they are given the necessary documents to immigrate to America. Uncle

Leo in Buffalo writes that he has borrowed $200 to pay for the Wolkowitzes' passage to the United States. For the first time since his early days in Brussels, David feels hope again.

Unfortunately, the U.S. government has strict immigration laws that allow only a certain number of immigrants to enter the country every month. So David and his mother are moved to the Les Milles transit camp, an abandoned brick factory near the city of Aix-en-Provence, to wait their turn.

Although conditions there aren't much better than in Rieucros, David finds one reason to be happy — he and his mother are reunited with Abraham, who also has been sent there. Not having seen his dad in nearly a year, the boy is shocked at Abraham's scrawny appearance. His father explains that at Gurs he had been mistreated and forced to work long hours for little food, and he saw hundreds of slave laborers fall dead from starvation and malnourishment.

Despite the priest's protection, David didn't feel too secure, because every week German troops stormed into Villard-de-Lans, randomly searching houses, hoping to flush out hidden Jews or members of the Resistance. During these raids, the priest concealed David behind a wall in the attic or had the boy mingle with the parishioners during Mass.

After a while, the Germans became suspicious of Monsieur le Curé's secret work helping Jews. Fearing that

David could be at risk staying with him, the priest arranged for the teen to work in exchange for room and board for Monsieur and Madame Pouteil-Noble, an elderly couple who needed help on their small farm. They treated David well and accepted the risks of harboring a Jew. Although he had been raised in a cultured life, he easily adapted to shoveling manure, tending the cows and pigs, and working the fields.

But even the countryside wasn't free from danger. The enemy staged surprise raids on farms, hunting for Jews and Resistance fighters. Whenever that happened, one farmer would run to the next farm to warn people that the Germans were coming. David would scurry into the mountain forest until the threat passed.

During one of those times, he encountered a group of Resistance fighters who wielded small weapons that had been parachuted to them by the British. The teenager revealed the truth to them about himself and his life.

"You could be a big help to us," the Resistance leader told him.

"How?"

"You could be a courier, relaying messages and information between the Resistance groups in the area — things such as the number of Germans who are coming our way, the kind of armament they're carrying, what they're riding in. Nothing is ever written down in case you are caught. But that won't be likely. You're young and shouldn't attract suspicion. You can still work on the farm. But we will need to get you a new identity."

David became the youngest member of the group. Three weeks later, the French underground gave him fake identification documents. From now on, he was Daniel Dumont.

Every morning at the Les Milles transit camp, David wakes up hoping, Is today the day they let us leave for America? And every night, when there was no word, he eases the disappointment by telling himself, Maybe tomorrow.

Rumors (which later turned out to be true) begin spreading in camp that anti-Semitic American officials, including Breckinridge Long, who is in charge of immigration for the U.S. State Department, are dragging their feet because they don't want more Jews in America.

Now it's early December 1941. Les Milles is buzzing with the stunning news that Japan has attacked Pearl Harbor, causing the United States to enter the war. "What does this mean, Pappi?" David asks Abraham.

"It means, son, that we won't be going to America."

The disheartened Wolkowitzes are shipped off to another camp, Rivesaltes, where men, women, and children are separated from one another by barbed-wire fences. The children are cared for by the OSE (Oeuvre de Secours aux Enfants), a French children's welfare society. Conditions are terrible and diseases, such as malaria and typhus, are rampant.

Now it's August 1942. Camp authorities order everyone to pack up their meager belongings and await transportation to "the East." Everyone assumes they will be resettled in a labor camp until the end of the war. The OSE convinces authorities that rather than go with their parents, the children will be safer in various orphanages that the welfare society operates throughout France.

David, who is 12, begs his parents, "Don't let them take me to an orphanage. I want to stay with you."

"It's for your own good," his mother says. "You'll be living in much better conditions. You'll have your own bed and lots of food. It'll be like a vacation."

"I'm afraid I won't see you again."

"Oh, don't worry," soothes his father. "We've been separated twice before and we ended up back together. This time, Mother and I will be gone until the war is over, and then we'll be a family once again."

David wants to believe him, but the boy sees in Abraham's eyes a haunting gaze that frightens him. It's the look of a man who doesn't believe his own words.

Regina hugs her son tighter than she has ever hugged him before and then steps away, sobbing. Abraham reaches for his cherished violin and gently runs his fingers over the rosewood. As tears trickle *down his cheeks, he hands it to David and says, "Take this. Keep it safe until we're together again."*

Gripping the violin, the heartbroken boy watches his parents get swallowed up by a mass of Jews who are being herded for shipment to "the East," wherever that is.

When he wasn't working on the farm, David was delivering messages for the Resistance. During one such mission, he was walking along a country road bordered by a deep ditch on each side. Without warning, a dozen German soldiers jumped out from the sides and ordered him to raise his hands. Once he got over the initial shock, he pretended not to understand them. *They'd become suspicious of me if I let on that I speak German,* he thought. He responded in French, "I don't understand what you are saying." None of the soldiers spoke French, so one of them motioned for him to raise his hands, which he did. His knees began to shake. *How am I ever going to get out of this mess?*

As they marched him toward the village, he understood every word they were saying to one another. What he heard petrified him. *They're taking me to Gestapo headquarters for questioning! They'll discover I'm a Jew, and then they'll torture and kill me!* He looked around, frantically searching for a way to escape, looking for someone who could help him. The only person he saw was the wife from the neighboring farm. She was standing in the field, showing no expression on her face as she watched David's arrest. *It's useless to try to escape,* he thought. He stared at the ground, resigned to his impending death. When he glanced into the field again, the woman had disappeared.

David was so scared he wondered how his legs could function, how his lungs could breathe. *How much time do I have left to live? When will they . . .*

Suddenly, gunfire erupted, and he fell to the ground. At first, he thought the soldiers were shooting at him, but then he realized that the bullets were coming from the edge of the woods next to the road. The soldiers scattered and leaped into the ditch on the opposite side. *Here's my chance!* He scrambled to his feet and sprinted into the woods, barely getting a glimpse of the Resistance fighters who had sprung him from certain death after the neighbor lady had alerted them.

He hurried back to the farm. Despite the scare, he continued to carry out his duties for the French Resistance. Conditions were primitive for the fighters. They slept on the ground and moved all the time. They couldn't light any fires at night for fear of being spotted by German patrols, so meals consisted of raw horse meat and raw eggs. David learned how to puncture an egg at both ends and then suck out the insides without breaking the shell.

With their parents shipped off to "the East," David and other boys from Les Milles are taken to an orphanage called Château Montintin, south of the French city of Limoges.

Although life at the orphanage is strictly regimented, the boys are well cared for. They receive adequate food, medical care, and an education, including carpentry classes and some religious instruction. They are kept busy, so they don't dwell on the war. Still, David cries himself to sleep every night because he misses his parents. He yearns for a letter from them—even one with blacked-out lines—but deep down he knows none will come. He has no idea where they are and he doubts they know where he is.

It's the summer of 1943. In spite of all the hardships the boys in the orphanage have endured, they never abandon their Jewish heritage. When David and five other boys near their thirteenth birthday, a rabbi is brought in from Limoges to prepare them for their bar mitzvah (the coming-of-age of a Jewish boy when he is responsible for his moral and religious duties). The bar mitzvah ceremony is held in a makeshift sanctuary of the orphanage. Each of the six boys is given an ink pen. What David wants most of all is to see his Mutti and Pappi. Not having them there at the ceremony—the most important day of a Jewish boy's life—makes his heart ache.

David's work with the Resistance ended after Allied forces drove the German army out of southern France in the summer of 1944. The OSE sent him to an orphanage in Montmorency, a suburb of Paris. Because he never forgot the address of his uncle Leo and aunt Golda—316

Commonwealth Avenue, Buffalo, New York, USA — he wrote to them. They responded by sending him care packages full of snacks and other treats.

When the war ended in 1945, David, like most people throughout the world, was horrified to learn that millions had been murdered in Nazi extermination camps. Hoping against hope that his parents were still alive, he contacted the International Red Cross and other refugee organizations that were trying to reunite survivors with their children.

While waiting for information about his parents, he wondered what it would be like to see them again. *How will I react? How much have they changed in my eyes? How much have I changed to them? It's been three years since we last saw one another. I'm no longer the little boy they remember. I'm fifteen now, and I've seen and suffered enough. But I survived. Maybe they have, too. Wouldn't it be wonderful to be a family again, to play music together again, to have a home again?*

David was eating lunch in the dining hall of the orphanage when an official came up to him and said, "We have news about your parents."

David took a deep breath and quickly studied the person's face, looking for a smile or a twinkle in the eyes that would tell him Abraham and Regina were alive.

"I'm sorry, David. They did not survive. They were killed in the gas chambers of Auschwitz in 1942."

Although he wasn't surprised, David still went numb. It was the tragic news he expected but didn't want to hear. He caught his breath and asked, "And my grandparents?"

22

"They were murdered in the Warsaw ghetto. My deepest sympathies."

I have nothing of my loved ones, David thought. *Not even Pappi's violin.* It had been left at Château Montintin for safekeeping and disappeared after he fled from the orphanage. *All I have are my memories.*

The heartbroken boy wrote to his aunt and uncle, who then set the wheels in motion to bring him to America. During the long wait, Leo's friend, U.S. Army Captain Irving Green, who was stationed in Paris, took David out to eat once a week.

One day, Green brought David to the American Consulate to see an official whose desk was stacked with files of people waiting to immigrate to America. Because the files were arranged alphabetically, David Wolkowitz's folder was near the bottom of the pile. "Do me a favor," Captain Green told the official. "David is an orphan. His parents were killed in Auschwitz. Put his file at the top so he can get to America. He's waited long enough."

When David, who had turned 16, arrived in Buffalo in 1946, Aunt Golda let him pour out his heart about the Holocaust. Then she gently cut him off, saying, "You have a new life now. Forget about everything that ever happened to you over there. Don't think about it. Don't even talk about it. You must move forward."

Over the next 50 years, he barely spoke about it. But every day since his arrival in America, David has vowed never to forget.

＝＝＝

Embraced by Leo and Golda Katz and their five children, David blossomed in high school in Buffalo. He eventually served in the U.S. Army in Germany as a member of a battalion that provided security for military trains. He married MaryAnne Vineberg in 1953, and they legally changed their last name to Katz in tribute to his aunt and uncle and cousins. David worked in the family concession business while he and MaryAnne raised four children. For 20 years, he sang with the Choral Arts Society and in the choir of the Buffalo Philharmonic. He retired in 1994 and moved to Chesapeake, Virginia, with his wife, an accomplished artist.

Since 1996, David Katz has been a member of the Holocaust Commission of the United Jewish Federation of Tidewater and speaks often to students and other groups. "I use my experiences during the Holocaust as an example of what happens when indifference, intolerance, lack of respect, and hate permeate our society," he says. "I speak to honor my parents, grandparents, and the six million other Jewish martyrs who perished during the Holocaust. I speak, because they can no longer speak."

"I'll Live to See You Pay for Your Crimes!"

===

Alicia Jurman

A licia Jurman trudged down the drab street, lugging two full water buckets that she had pumped from the well in the bleak Jewish ghetto in Buczacz (pronounced BOO-chatch), Poland. Her heavy coat and the thick shawl that was wrapped over her nose and mouth warded off the stinging December wind. Her arm bore a white band with an embroidered blue Star of David.

She had aged much over the past three years, ever since her country was invaded by Nazi Germany in 1939. Heartache will do that to a child. A girl of 12, Alicia had suffered enough pain to last a lifetime. Many lifetimes. Three of her brothers had been murdered, and her father was missing and feared dead.

Now, in 1942, all that remained of the once proud and well-off Jurman family were Alicia, her brother Herzl, 10, and their mother, Frieda. They lived in one room of a house in the dreary ghetto that held 18,000 Jews in a county of 80,000 people. And they lived in terror. Two months earlier, the Germans had seized 2,000 Jews in the ghetto and killed them. As young as she was, Alicia made a vow to herself to do everything within her power to protect her mother and little brother.

Moments after Alicia entered the hall in her home and put down the water buckets, she heard a harsh rap at the front door. Opening it, she faced a steely-eyed policeman who read off her mother's name from a small notebook he was holding. "Frieda Jurman?" he asked.

First they came for the fathers, and now they've come for the mothers, she thought. *Well, they can't take mine!* Alicia, who was tall for her age, was still clad in her shawl and coat so that only her eyes could be seen. *Can I make him think I'm Mama?*

"Are you Frieda Jurman?" he repeated sternly.

She nodded.

"Come with me."

Her nerves slithering in fear, Alicia followed him in the snow to the police station. She said nothing, afraid that her childlike voice would give her away. Thrown into a cell with grown women, the girl curled up in a ball in the corner, fearing the worst. The next morning, each prisoner was ordered to sign his or her name at the desk of a

Ukrainian policeman. (Thousands of Ukrainian policemen and authorities worked for the Nazis.) While standing in line, Alicia gasped because she recognized the policeman as the father of her close friend Olga, a man who had always treated Alicia with affection. *How can he collaborate with the Germans?* she thought. *He's nothing but a traitor!*

When it was her turn to write her name, Alicia, now seething mad, wrote in bold, angry strokes, "Alicia Jurman."

When the policeman looked up, he said with surprise, "Alicia, what are you doing here?"

"I was brought here with the others."

He motioned for her to come closer because he didn't want anyone else to hear him. "There must be a mistake," he whispered. "This *Aktion* [the German word for the rounding up of Jews for deportation or murder] wasn't meant for children like you, only adults. The soldiers will be here soon and take you away unless you do as I say. When they come, get down on your knees and beg for your life."

She scowled at him and turned away.

When the soldiers arrived, they began loading up the prisoners into sleighs bound for another snow-covered city. With eyes wide and a nod, Olga's father signaled Alicia to kneel and plead to the soldiers. She responded with a defiant stare. *I will never beg for my life! Never!* she told herself. *It won't do any good to beg. They're heartless murdering Nazis. Even if they released me, they'd go after Mama.*

As Alicia was being led away, Olga's father rushed over and slapped her across the face, staggering her. Then he struck her again, sending her backpedaling into the line. He glared at her but said nothing. She knew exactly why he hit her: *He's lashing out from his own guilt and frustrated that I won't try to save myself. He's angry that he'll have my death on his conscience. Well, that gives me some satisfaction. The traitor!*

She and the others were taken 20 miles to a prison in nearby Chortkov, Poland (also called Czortkow and today known as Chortkiv, Ukraine), where the Gestapo had its regional headquarters. When the captives arrived, S.S. men barked orders and insults, yanking people off the sleighs and beating them with sticks and rifle butts.

Seeing a woman fall from a blow to the neck, Alicia helped her to her feet. But this act of kindness infuriated an S.S. man, who whacked Alicia so hard with a bamboo ski pole that it knocked the breath out of her. He beat her again and again until the pole snapped in two and she crumpled to the ground. "Dirty Jew!" he screamed, kicking her with his heavy boots until she heard several ribs crack.

A captive who was a family friend helped walk the injured girl into the prison. All the women were ordered to take off their winter coats and throw them in a pile and remove all their jewelry. When Alicia couldn't get an earring off fast enough, an S.S. officer angrily yanked it off, tearing her earlobe.

As blood flowed down her cheek, Alicia fearlessly berated him. "How dare you call yourself an officer," she snapped. "My father was a decorated hero in World War One and an officer and a gentleman. You are a disgrace to the uniform."

Releasing her anger felt good—until the S.S. officer and his comrades brutally beat her and kicked her into unconsciousness. She woke up in terrible pain the next morning in a crowded, freezing cell.

Soon guards charged in and randomly took away eight women. From a courtyard-facing window, which was too high to see out of, Alicia heard growling dogs and women shrieking in terror. Alicia wanted to put her hands over her ears to muffle the horrible sounds, but it hurt too much to touch her torn ear.

For two days, prisoners were dragged out to the courtyard and attacked by the snarling dogs. Some of the ravaged inmates were returned to the cell, their arms and legs torn. Others never came back. Alicia didn't need to ask about them. She knew they were dead.

Scrunched in a corner of the dank cell, she tried to sleep to ease the pain and shut out the screams. Even when she couldn't sleep, she kept her eyes closed because she couldn't stand to look at the Nazis' faces.

On the third day, a guard brought in a bucket of water and told the inmates, "Drink all you want." Not having eaten or drunk since her imprisonment, Alicia and the others eagerly slurped down the cold water. They were given as much as they wanted—but no food.

Soon everyone, including Alicia, became sick. Many were dying from illness. Feverish, weak, and starving, the teenager could feel her life slipping away. She was among the living dead, almost numb to her pain, fear, and sorrow. *Just let go,* she told herself.

The girl was fading fast when, from deep within herself, she felt an intense spirit that brightened by the minute. *I won't let you kill me! I'll show you. I won't die. I'll live to see you pay for your crimes!*

Then she lapsed into a coma.

When Alicia awakened, she found herself in a comfortable bed in a darkened room. She was sweating and shivering. Her joints and head ached, and her lungs hurt with every breath. She was too feeble to even roll over.

Her eyes focused on the smiling faces of attorney Jules Gold and his wife, Sala. They told her she had been in a coma for 14 days and that they had been caring for her in their home in Chortkov's Jewish ghetto.

"It doesn't seem possible that I could be unconscious for two weeks," she mumbled. "How did I get here? What happened to me?"

"You're in my home because I discovered you in a pile of dead bodies at the prison cemetery," Mr. Gold replied. "The Germans force Jews like me to bury people who died in prison. Apparently, you had passed out in your cell, and the guards assumed you were dead and threw you onto the stack of bodies for burial.

"When I picked you up, I heard you moan and then I realized that your body was warm. We pretended to bury you and actually put you in a grave, but in such a way that you could still breathe. When the guards left, we pulled you out. I wrapped you in my coat and hid you under the straw in my sleigh and brought you here. We've been caring for you ever since."

After Mrs. Gold brought her a bowl of thin, watery soup, Alicia said, "I hurt all over. What's wrong with me?"

"Besides the awful beatings you were given?" Mr. Gold replied. "You're suffering from typhoid fever, but the worst is over. The Germans gave you contaminated water to drink."

"Did everyone else in prison die?"

"No, some prisoners were released and sent back to Buczacz so they would bring the disease with them and unknowingly pass it on to others."

"It's not enough that the Nazis torture and beat us to death," Alicia said. "Now they're trying to kill us by disease, too."

She stayed in bed for about a month while the Golds nursed her back to health, sharing what little soup and bread they could obtain in the ghetto. During that time, Alicia told them the story of her young life.

Born into an upper-class family with four brothers, she became competitive and athletic, earning medals in track and swim meets. Her father, Sigmund, a successful businessman, and her mother, Frieda, a violet-eyed, cultured lady, raised Alicia to be assertive and resourceful and have a love of the outdoors and school.

When war came to Buczacz (now known as Buchach, Ukraine), the girl's heart was soon ripped to shreds. Her eldest brother, Moshe, died in prison. Her father was one of the city's 600 Jewish civic, business, and religious leaders who disappeared after the Nazis took them away, probably to their deaths; no one knew for sure. Then the Germans shipped her brother Bunio to a labor camp. When a fellow prisoner escaped, the Nazis punished the rest by lining up all the inmates and killing every tenth prisoner. Bunio was a tenth prisoner. Fueled by a seething hatred of Nazis, her brother Zachary, 17, fought for the underground until he was betrayed by a Polish so-called friend and hanged in front of the police station.

"All I have left are my mother and my younger brother, Herzl, back in the ghetto in Buczacz," she told the Golds.

On the first day that Alicia got out of bed, Mrs. Gold gave her a pair of boy's pants and a shirt to wear. "They were our son's," the woman explained. "The Germans killed him shortly before you came to stay with us."

Alicia wobbled over to Mrs. Gold and hugged her. "I'm very sorry for your loss."

"I'm sure he would have liked you very much," said Mrs. Gold, breaking down.

"I wish I could have met him. He was probably just as caring as you and Mr. Gold. I'm so grateful for everything you've done for me. I'll never forget you. If I didn't have a mother and brother waiting for me, I would stay with you. But I'm committed to keeping them alive."

Six weeks after her rescue, Mr. Gold arranged for Alicia to be smuggled out of the Chortkov ghetto. She hid in a box under a bed of straw in the back of a peasant's sleigh. When she returned to the Buczacz ghetto, she saw signs on the front doors, including her family's, warning that the occupants inside were suffering from typhoid. *The Germans' plan worked*, she thought, a wave of disgust crashing over her. Inside, she found her mother and Herzl lying in their beds, sick and barely conscious.

Seeing Alicia, Frieda smiled weakly and uttered, "Alicia, you have come home to us."

"Yes, Mama, I have come home."

Alicia, with the help of her close friend Milek, a boy two years older than her, provided the loving care that pulled Frieda and Herzl back from the brink of death. But the lack of food was a major problem. The Jurmans had no money because Frieda had given it all to the Germans as ransom for the safe return of her husband — a promise that the Nazis had no intention of keeping.

While worrying over how they would survive, Alicia pulled out from her jacket a small package from Mrs. Gold that the girl had forgotten about. She opened it and let out a whoop. Inside was enough money to last the Jurmans through the winter. The accompanying note from Mrs. Gold said, "This is my son's money, which he normally carried with him in his jacket so that he could try to buy his life if he were caught. When he was caught, he wasn't wearing his jacket."

Tears filled Alicia's eyes. *If by some miracle I live through this and I'm free again, I'll be like a daughter to the*

Golds. I will love them and care for them with all my heart.

Over the next few months, the Gestapo carried out several *Aktionen* that nearly wiped out the ghetto until it was decreed that Buczacz would become *Judenrein*, German for "free of all Jews." The survivors—who, like the Jurmans, had hidden in their homemade hideouts during the *Aktionen*—were forced to move to a different Jewish ghetto, this one in the city of Kopechince (pronounced Ko-pa-CHIN-say).

Before they left, Milek and Alicia spent a few tender moments together outside her home. Milek was orphaned after his parents were killed by the Germans, but despite his young age, he took care of himself. He hoped to be a doctor when he grew up.

"I'll be going to Kopechince later and I'll see you there," he told Alicia. "But first . . ." He took her hand and placed a small gold band in her palm. "It was my mother's wedding ring. I want you to have this." Closing her fingers over the ring, he said, "Take good care of it."

Alicia gazed into his blue eyes and melted. Even though she was only 13, she was deeply in love with him, but she didn't have the courage to tell him. He kissed her on the cheek and left. *I won't let the Germans take it away from me,* she promised herself. She wrapped the ring in her handkerchief and placed it behind a loose stone in the rock wall of the backyard. *I'll come back for it someday.*

In Kopechince, Alicia and her mother and brother moved into a six-room house that eventually held five other families, including two babies. The Jurmans lived in the kitchen, where it was the warmest. Shortly after getting settled, the families were warned of another *Aktion*. The house had a secret bunker in the cellar, but it wasn't big enough for everyone, so they decided that only the adults and young children would hide in it. The older children—two boys and Alicia—were told to take cover in the attic or in a nearby meadow. The two babies weren't allowed in the bunker out of fear that if they cried, they would give everyone away when the Germans searched the house. The infants, who were given drugged tea so they would sleep, were hidden in a bedroom.

After the families entered the bunker, Alicia kissed her mother and Herzl, closed the lid, and covered it with household junk, old clothing, and potato sacks. She made sure not to disturb the dust on the lid because sharp-eyed Nazis looked for fresh fingerprints and smudges to find concealed bunkers.

The boys dashed out of the house to hide while Alicia scrambled for the attic. On her way, she heard the infants cry. *I can't leave the babies alone,* she thought. *I have to try to quiet them.* She scurried into the infants' room and fed them chamomile tea so they would go back to sleep.

Alicia was almost finished when the S.S. men and Ukrainian police burst into the house, overturning furniture and shouting, "Out, dirty Jews, out!"

Her first instinct was to flee, but she wouldn't leave the babies, who now were wailing from all the commotion.

What can I do? Where can I . . . Before Alicia could complete her thought, two Germans charged into the room. One of them pistol-whipped her and shoved her out of the house. As she was led away, she heard gunshots.

Using their rifle butts as prods, soldiers and police herded hundreds of Jews, including Alicia, into a prison courtyard, where they were kept overnight. Word spread that the ghetto in Kopechince was being liquidated. *The Aktion will continue until everyone is killed,* Alicia worried. *What will happen to Mama and Herzl and Milek? I have to stop thinking about them, or I'll lose my mind.*

The next morning, German soldiers began selecting groups of Jews and forcing them at gunpoint to walk toward the forest. The captives all knew that when they reached their destination, their lives would end. Alicia's turn came around noon. On her death march, she saw fellow Jews stagger and stumble. The slower people who fell or stopped to rest—mostly older ones—were shot on the spot. The farther she walked, the more fresh bodies she saw along the side of the road.

Finally, her group arrived at a clearing where a large pit had been dug. The soldiers shoved several Jews up to the front and then shot them. The victims toppled dead into the pit. With a gun barrel poking in her back, Alicia was pushed forward with other Jews. Believing she had only seconds left to live, she chose to picture in her mind her mother and brother. She wanted them to be the last mental images of her short life.

All of a sudden she heard machine-gun fire, but it wasn't

coming from behind her. Someone was shooting from the side. Over the roar she heard a familiar voice call out her name. "Alicia Jurman! Run, Alicia!" She turned and saw Milek firing a machine gun at the stunned Germans. "Run! Run!" he shouted to her, still spraying the soldiers with bullets.

Alicia pushed her way through the screaming horde of victims, who were fleeing in all directions, and sprinted into the forest. She kept running for more than an hour until she collapsed deep in the woods. Her mind flooded with worry. *Did the Germans find Mama and Herzl? What happened to the babies? And Milek, brave Milek. What a courageous act. How could he possibly survive against all those Germans?* The horrors that she had experienced over the past 24 hours consumed her. On her knees, the girl sobbed uncontrollably until she was so drained she fell asleep.

When Alicia woke up the next morning, she didn't dare return to Kopechince. Instead, she headed for her hometown of Buczacz, because her mother had told her and Herzl that if they were ever separated to go there and wait to be reunited.

Posing as an orphaned peasant girl, Alicia spent two weeks working in various farmers' fields for food on the way to Buczacz. When she arrived, she waited until dark before approaching her house, because she was worried that a Nazi-sympathizing neighbor would capture and kill her.

Not finding her mother hiding at home, Alicia went to the wall in the backyard where she had hidden her most precious possession—the ring that Milek had given her.

After what she had been through, she wanted to wear it so she could feel close to him. Groping in the dark, she found the loose stone that hid the ring and pulled it out. Slipping the ring on her finger, she thought, *I want Milek to always be with me if only in spirit. He's the reason I'm still alive. I hope they didn't kill him. No, I'm going to believe that he's alive. He probably has no idea that I'm in love with him. He probably thinks of me as just a close friend. And that's all right. I'll cherish this ring forever.*

Later that night, she went to the home of her non-Jewish neighbors, Mr. and Mrs. Orlovski. It was a big gamble, but she thought she could trust them. After they got over the shock of her presence, she asked if they had seen her mother or brother.

"Of course not," said Mr. Orlovski. "There are no more Jews in Buczacz. The city is *Judenrein*."

After Alicia described the Kopechince massacre and how she had escaped, the couple gave her a small bundle of food and sent her on her way. Alicia needed shelter close to town while she waited for her mother. Borrowing a shovel from a toolshed on a farmer's field, she dug a bunker and covered it with straw. She slept there, taking three or four nibbles of bread each day to ward off the hunger.

On the morning of the eighth day, she woke up to the sound of children's voices. Then, without warning, her straw bunker collapsed because someone walked on it. Alicia climbed out and was astonished to see her school friend Lala and Lala's two cousins, Josek and Sosia, whose family owned the land.

"What are you doing here?" Lala asked.

"I'm hiding," Alicia replied. "You know what's happening to Jews. I'm trying to survive."

During the girls' conversation, Josek turned ugly and demanded that Alicia give him her ring. When she refused, he snarled, "The owner of this land doesn't know you're here, does he?"

Josek is threatening to turn me in, Alicia thought. *I should fight him. No, he's stronger than I am. Even if I do fight him for the ring, he'll get the police and they'll come for me and look for other Jews who might be hiding out here. I can't do that to them. Milek, forgive me.* Reluctantly, she handed him the ring, saying, "It's all I have left in the world."

After examining it, Josek announced, "This is real gold. I can get some money for this."

"Give it back to her, Josek," Lala pleaded. He refused and walked away. Turning toward Alicia but unable to look her in the eye, Lala said, "I'm sorry, Alicia. Good-bye. We won't tell anyone where you are. I promise."

Hurt and angry, Alicia mumbled to herself, *I haven't met one Pole who will stand up for a Jew.* Knowing she could no longer stay in her bunker, Alicia headed in the opposite direction, her vision blurred by the flood of tears that wouldn't stop flowing.

That night, she lay down at the bottom of a little ravine and fell asleep and dreamed that the ghost of her mother was hovering over her. "Are you dead, Mama?" the girl asked in her dream. "Is that what you're trying to tell me?" The ghost answered, "Alicia, it's Mama. Wake up, sweetheart. It's Mama."

Alicia opened her eyes and saw her mother, who seemed so real.

"Alicia, it's Mama."

"It really *is* you!" Alicia charged into her mother's arms and sobbed like a baby. She held her tight, not able to say a word for the longest time. When she was finally able to speak, Alicia asked, "What happened to you in Kopechince?"

"We hid for three days in the bunker and then came out," Frieda replied. "Herzl learned that you were part of the death march, and we feared you were dead. But I couldn't know for certain unless Herzl and I went to Buczacz to look for you. On the day we were to leave, I couldn't find him anywhere. I waited for three days, but when I heard the Germans were starting another *Aktion*, I left for Buczacz."

"But how did you find me?"

"I stopped at the Orlovskis', and they told me you had been to their house only two days before me. For nearly a week, I've been roaming the fields, calling out your name and searching for you. Yesterday, I was hiding in a ravine when I overheard a girl arguing with a boy over a ring that he had taken from her friend Alicia. When I heard your name, I knew you had to be nearby. I searched all through the night. And now I've found you."

As she lay in her mother's arms, Alicia thought, *Sometimes you are forced to give up something dear to you, and you don't know the reason for it. I had to give up my ring, but it led Mama to me.*

Alicia and her mother formed a plan for survival while living in the fields and ravines. During the day, the girl would seek work on farms, asking to be paid with food while Frieda hid. The farms were located in a region that Poland had annexed from its neighbor the Ukraine after World War I. A resistance group of Ukrainian nationalists known as the Bandera sided with the Nazis and hoped that if Germany won the war, the region would become part of an independent Ukraine. To advance the German cause—and, therefore, their own self-interests—the Bandera willingly hunted and killed Jews. Because some farms were owned by Ukrainians and some by Poles, Alicia—who spoke Polish and Ukrainian as well as German and Russian—had two different fake stories about her life, depending on the farmer's nationality.

With her braided hair and bandanna, Alicia looked and acted like a hardworking peasant girl. Although she didn't want to attract attention, she couldn't help herself while toiling in a particular wheat field for several days. She noticed a strapping 17-year-old boy named Pietro, whose father owned the land. He liked to sing while he worked in the field—and so did Alicia. Although the two never actually spoke to each other, they communicated by singing songs from opposite ends of the field. It was one of the few times she enjoyed her work.

Eventually, Alicia befriended an elderly man whom villagers feared was possessed by demons when, in fact, he suffered from epileptic seizures. The man, a beekeeper who sold honey, had already taken in a Jewish mother and her two children and agreed to let Alicia and Frieda stay, too. His house was a perfect place for the Jews to live because no one dared go near his property out of fear of his "demons." The women and children affectionately called him *Wujciu,* Polish for "uncle" and pronounced VOOY-choo. The household grew larger after Alicia rescued another Jewish mother with two children. They had been hiding in the fields from the deadly Bandera, who were coming to kill them.

There was barely enough food to keep all eight in Wujciu's house from starving to death. During the potato harvest, Alicia began secretly leaving potatoes along the edges of the fields and covering them with discarded stalks. When it grew dark, she would return, collect them, and take them home, where they were carefully rationed.

One day, Wujciu went into Buczacz to ask Alicia's trusted school friend Slavka for clothing. He returned with shoes, a coat, and other goods—and also the worst news imaginable: "Your brother Herzl is dead," he told Alicia. His words struck with such force that she nearly fainted and he had to catch her. "I am so sorry, Alicia. Slavka said that your brother was pointed out to the police by a former school friend, a boy who knew him well. Herzl was taken out and shot."

The girl shook from excruciating despair. *Now I have to tell Mama that her last son was murdered just like all her other sons.* She dropped to the ground, beat her fists on the hard earth, and howled like a dog. As much as her heart ached for Herzl, it hurt even more for her mother.

During December 1943, the families in Wujciu's home were startled one night by loud pounding on the door. "Open up, Jews!" a voice barked in Ukrainian. "We know you're in there! Open up or we'll break in the door!"

Everyone in the house scurried into the back storage room and dived under cut straw. But Alicia realized it offered little sanctuary, so she got up, closed the storage door behind her, and with her heart beating wildly, opened the front door. She stared into the stern faces of six young men wearing blue caps, which signified they were members of the hated Bandera. "Where are you hiding the Jews?" one of them demanded.

Suddenly, Pietro entered the room. Surprised to see Alicia, he said, "What are you doing here with the Jews?"

All at once, Alicia was no longer afraid. The fury inside her began to churn. "You want to know what I am doing with the Jews, Pietro? Because I *am* a Jew!"

His mouth dropped open. "But that can't be . . ."

"Have you come to take us to the police, or will you just kill us right here?" She stepped closer and glared at him. "I am a Jew and I have a right to live just like you.

I am thirteen years old, and I'm doing everything I can to stay alive. Now you and your friends want to kill innocent women and children."

She clenched her fists and raised her voice, addressing all of the young Bandera. "Someday you will marry and have children and then you'll know what it is to live in fear, because there will come a time when you will feel my curse. I swear in the name of my God and your God, I will haunt you from my grave. You won't know a day's happiness, any of you!"

Without a word, Pietro turned to his friends, motioned them to leave, and gently closed the door behind him. Only then did she start to shake. Although there was no guarantee that the Bandera would leave them alone, the Jews decided to stay with Wujciu. It was either that or freeze to death in the woods.

Weeks later, Alicia met a middle-aged Jewish man who was hiding in an underground room in a barn. During their conversation, he revealed that he was one of the 600 missing Jewish leaders in Buczacz whom the Germans had rounded up.

Alicia's mind began to spin. *Could he possibly know what happened to Papa? Is it possible that Papa is alive?* Her voice quaking with anticipation, she asked, "What happened to all of you?"

"The Germans took us into prison cells and early the following morning they marched us to the Fador [a large meadow by the river] and then . . ." His voice began to crack. Regaining his composure, he continued, "And then the shooting started. I ran and was shot in the leg, but I kept going. I escaped."

"Did anyone else escape?" she asked hopefully.

He shook his head. "Only me. But there was one man I thought would make it. The German soldier who was going to shoot him saw that the man was wearing a World War One medal for bravery from the Austrian emperor. The soldier was impressed enough to let him escape and told him to run. But a Ukrainian policeman shot him in the back."

Alicia's mouth went dry. *Papa always wore his medal for bravery.* "What did the man look like?"

"Tall, handsome, reddish-blond hair."

He's describing Papa! Alicia left the barn in a daze, trembling all the way back to Wujciu's. *It's confirmed. There is now only Mama and me. I can't tell Mama about Papa. She has suffered enough.*

That night, Alicia cried out in her sleep, waking up her mother. "What's troubling you, sweetheart?" Frieda asked.

"Sometimes I feel this war will never end."

Stroking the girl's hair, Frieda cooed, "Everything that has a beginning must have an end. Besides, we must have faith."

Two months later, on March 24, 1944, Frieda's faith was confirmed. The Russians ousted the Germans and liberated the region. That evening, an ecstatic Alicia and the others at Wujciu's celebrated by eating honey and bread. "We're free!" she declared. Soon she and her mother said good-bye to the kindhearted man who provided them and the other Jews with shelter for eight difficult months. The Jurmans hitched a ride on a Russian soldier's sleigh and rode the 25 miles to Buczacz. Along the way, people waved and blew kisses to the advancing Russian army.

The excitement over returning to her hometown faded when Alicia saw unsmiling Polish neighbors—the same ones who had betrayed Jews and looted their homes. What was she really going back to? She and her mother had no home (it belonged to someone else now), no possessions, and no family. As one of 250 Jews who returned—out of nearly 18,000 murdered—she, like each survivor, was filled with a terrible sense of loss and sadness.

After Frieda found them a three-room apartment, they tried to settle into a new life. During those first few nights, Frieda would wait until Alicia was asleep before releasing her grief over the deaths of her loved ones. But her silent sobbing was so deep that the bed she shared with Alicia would shake and wake the girl up.

Alicia took daily walks through the streets of Buczacz, recognizing other survivors by their undernourished bodies and pale faces. One day, she approached the police station, where she had been processed for prison by her friend Olga's father. Glancing through a window into the prison yard, she saw the police burning stacks of papers and official files. *Probably the German records of all the Jews who were arrested,* she thought. *Is the name Sigmund Jurman on one of those lists? Or Zachary's or Bunio's or Herzl's . . . or even mine?*

"Alicia! Alicia!"

The moment she heard that voice—that warm and wonderful voice—her heart danced. She spun on her heels and saw a boy running down the street toward her. "Milek!" she yelled, and rushed toward him.

Deliriously happy that the other was alive, they hugged and kissed and cried for several minutes before either could say a word. Then both started babbling at the same time.

"You saved my life in Kopechince," she said. "I was so worried you were killed. How did you ever manage to pull off such a brave attack against all those Germans?"

"I snuck up behind a soldier, hit him, and stole his machine gun. Before the Germans could react, I fired off dozens of rounds. By the time they started shooting back, I had fled into the woods. I hoped you and others had escaped, but I didn't know if you made it."

The thrilled girl brought Milek to see her mother, who invited him to move in with them, but as tempting as the offer was, he felt compelled to leave the next day to search for relatives in his hometown of Stanislawów.

Two months after the Russians liberated the region, the Jewish survivors were settling into a sense of normalcy. Alicia was starting to feel safe again, relieved that she wouldn't have to face another vicious Nazi. She was finally sleeping through the night with fewer nightmares, until . . .

KA-BOOM! KA-BOOM! Thundering explosions in the distance jolted Alicia and her mother awake in the middle of the night. Alicia recognized the sounds of the blasts. "Artillery shells!"

The two of them threw on their clothes and rushed outside, smack into a whirlwind of panic. Fleeing Russian troops and civilians surged through streets clogged with trucks, horses, and wagons.

Alicia collared a young soldier and asked, "What's going on?"

"We had trapped the German divisions, but they broke through our lines and are fighting their way back to Germany — right through Buczacz!"

Alicia felt as though she had been clubbed over the head. Her whole body stiffened and then quivered so badly she could hardly stand. *The Germans are coming back! The nightmare has returned!*

Trying to reach shelter in the ruins of a nearby castle, Alicia and her mother pushed their way through a sea of terrified people who didn't know which way to run, because fierce shelling was blasting the city from the north, east, and south. Suddenly, a deafening blast from an artillery shell exploded in front of them, its impact throwing Alicia to the ground. As she picked herself up, she heard men, women, and children shrieking in agony and saw bodies slumped on the street and sidewalks. "Mama! Mama!" she cried out.

A few yards away, Alicia found her mother, who was

gripping her bloody leg. "I've been hit in the thigh by shrap-nel," Frieda said, her face contorted in pain.

Alicia helped her to a nearby field where she ripped her dress to make bandages. She wrapped her mother's leg as tightly as she could, but within seconds the bandages were soaked through. "Mama, let's try to get back home."

With the last ounce of her strength, Frieda limped back to their apartment, where Alicia nursed her day and night. However, without medicine, the wound became infected. Frieda begged Alicia to flee the city and stay at Wujciu's, but the girl refused. "I will never leave you alone, Mama."

"You must go, Alicia. You must live and, to live, you must hide. You owe it to all of us to survive. You are the only wit-ness to what has happened to our family, to our people."

"But you are a witness, too."

"I will not survive this war."

Alicia remained with her mother behind their locked door for a week after the Germans reoccupied the city. Then came the sounds they dreaded most—a loud knock and a gruff voice ordering, "Jews, outside now!"

"One of our neighbors must have squealed on us," Alicia moaned.

Frieda was too weak to move. There was no time to hide. So they clutched each other, their stomachs twisting in knots, and watched two large S.S. men kick the door off its hinges and storm inside. "Out! Make it quick, Jews!" they hollered.

With Alicia propping up her mother, they went out into the street, which was deserted. As Frieda clung to Alicia, one of the S.S. men stepped back, drew his pistol, and aimed it right at the girl's head. *He's going to kill me now,* she thought, *but I'm no longer afraid.* For a split second, she saw a look pass between the gunman and her mother—an unspoken exchange. Then Alicia closed her eyes and waited for the bullet to snuff out her life.

The gun went off with a loud bang. Alicia's body jerked, but she felt nothing. She opened her eyes. *I'm still alive!* Then she let out a howl that erupted from the core of her being. There at her feet lay her mother. Dead. Frieda had thrown herself between the gun and Alicia, taking the bullet meant for her daughter.

While Alicia reeled in sorrow, the enraged S.S. man pointed his pistol at her again. He cocked his weapon and squeezed the trigger. *Click.* He cocked it again and fired. *Click. He's run out of bullets. He used the last one on Mama.*

For some unknown reason, neither S.S. man made another attempt to kill Alicia. Instead they pushed her forward, but not before she took one last glimpse of her mother's body. *Good-bye, Mama. I love you.*

Alicia was taken to the same police station as before, but she didn't see Olga's father this time. Put in a cell designed for 4 people but now holding 25, Alicia leaned against the cold wall and studied the gloomy faces of her fellow Jews. She spotted Eva, a good friend of her brother Zachary, and talked to her. Once a beautiful girl, Eva was pitifully thin with a sallow face and dull eyes rimmed by dark rings. She spoke slowly and cast a distant gaze.

Alicia said, "The Gestapo will take us all to the Fador in the morning and shoot us. But I know how we can escape.

"When they line us up, we need to be on the far end. Once the shooting starts, we must run from the group and get to the river. There's a large tree in the water that I found a few years ago. From the outside, it looks like an ordinary tree. But it's hollow. You can enter the inside of the tree by diving below the surface and going through a large hole in the trunk. There's plenty of air when you resurface in it. Because the tree is in the water, the dogs won't smell us. It's a perfect place to hide."

Still not looking at Alicia, Eva hesitated and then in a monotone voice asked, "What if something goes wrong and we're caught?"

"What does it matter? They'll kill us anyway."

When Alicia woke up the next morning, she found Eva barely responsive. She was staring off into the distance and not speaking. Trying to snap her out of her stupor, Alicia slapped and shook her, but Eva's head nodded limply from side to side. Alicia could tell that there was no life in Eva's eyes. *She's lost her mind. She doesn't know where she is or what's about to happen. She's obviously separated her mind from her body so she doesn't have to suffer anymore. I must still try to save her.* "Just stay with me, Eva, and we'll escape together."

Moments later, German guards ordered everyone out of the cell. Eva held Alicia's hand when the girls joined about 200 Jews who had been rounded up by the Gestapo. "Our neighbors turned us in again," Alicia muttered angrily.

The Jews were marched toward the Fador just as Alicia had expected. When they arrived, she saw a long, narrow, open grave. The S.S. men ordered everyone to line up side by side directly in front of it. Alicia moved to the far end, having learned from her escape during the Kopechince massacre. "Remember to run to the river and look for the hollow tree," she whispered to Eva, who was still holding her hand. Eva gave no indication that she heard her.

The second Alicia heard the first shot, she tried to flee, but Eva held tightly to Alicia's hand and wouldn't move. "Come on!" Alicia yelled, jerking at her hand. "Run!" Eva kept staring forward, her hand in an iron grip. Machine-gun fire was mowing people down. *I've got to get loose or I'll die!* With one desperate tug, Alicia pulled her hand free and bolted. She zigzagged in a swath of bullets, trying to make it harder for the S.S. men to shoot her. Others were fleeing, too, in the mayhem.

Despite her weakened condition from malnutrition, Alicia scampered down to the river. Just as her legs were giving out, she plunged into the cold water and stayed below the surface, coming up for air only once. Her pencil-thin arms burned as she feverishly stroked her way to the hollow tree, swam through the underwater opening, and then broke the surface inside the tree. Gasping, she thought, *I'm safe—at least for now.*

She remained concealed in the tree all day, unable to stop shivering from cold and fear. Outside she heard muffled shouts, barking dogs, and occasional gunfire. *I wonder how many escaped like me.* Late that night, she left the tree, swam across the river, climbed out, and headed into the forest, chilled and wet. *I need to find shelter and dry clothes, or I could end up dead.*

Stopping at the first farm she reached, she slipped into a barn, took off her clothes, squeezed out the water, and laid them out to dry. Then she wrapped herself in empty potato sacks and tried to sleep. But she tossed and turned. Whenever she closed her eyes, she relived all the horror of the last two days: her harrowing escape, the attempted curbside execution, and, most painfully of all, her mother's ultimate sacrifice.

Those same frightening images returned night after night, robbing her of any rest as she wandered aimlessly through the forest over the next two weeks. Without sleep, her fighting spirit and physical strength dwindled, and the emotional pain from her grief mushroomed. The girl secured just enough food from refugees and farmers to stay alive, but she was a shell of her former self, a forlorn orphan who had no plan, no hope.

Surrendering to exhaustion one night, she collapsed to the ground and finally fell into a deep sleep. Once again she dreamed about her mother, but this time she dreamed that

Frieda was alive. "Get up, Alicia," Frieda called. "Get up off the ground. You must not lie there and grieve. You must go on living. You must live, Alicia, you must live!"

Alicia woke up with a start. Rays from the morning sun had filtered their way through the trees and reached the forest floor. She felt a warmth not from the sunbeams but rather, she was sure, from her mother's spirit. Feeling as though Frieda's arms were comforting her, Alicia unleashed all her pent-up sorrow, torment, and misery in choking sobs until there was nothing left to vent.

The long, hard cry made her feel better. She rose to her feet with renewed grit and courage. The girl who had escaped death so many times before now knew, absolutely knew, that she would survive. *I will live!*

═══

Alicia Jurman worked in the fields for food until liberation a few months later. Twice during that time she saved the lives of Russian partisans by warning them of nearby German forces and providing them food. For her efforts, she was awarded a medal and made an honorary lieutenant by the Russian partisans.

After the war, she felt more heartache when she learned that her dear friend Milek had been killed when he stepped on a German land mine. She was never able to locate Mr. and Mrs. Gold to find out their fate.

With no family of her own, Alicia began caring for Jewish orphans who had survived the death camps.

She also worked with the underground organization Brekha, which smuggled out Jews who were trapped behind the Iron Curtain (the political border of countries under Soviet communist control). Eventually, she immigrated to Israel. During Israel's War of Independence, she served in the navy, sometimes in combat.

In 1950, she married Gabriel Appleman, an American engineer who was working in Haifa, Israel. Two years later, they moved to the United States, where she began a lifelong quest to educate herself through college courses.

Since 1963 — after the birth of the youngest of her three children — Alicia has devoted her time to educating people of all ages about the Holocaust. She has spoken in grade schools, high schools, colleges, synagogues, churches, and conferences. She spent three years writing her book Alicia: My Story — *a gripping account of her life during and immediately after the Holocaust — which Bantam Books published in 1988.*

Today, Alicia Appleman-Jurman — a widowed grandmother who lives in San Jose, California — conducts teleconferences to classrooms about the Holocaust. Says Alicia, "I pray that Jew and non-Jew alike unite in the resolve that evil forces will never again be permitted to set one people against another."

"Mama, It's the Gas Chamber!"

===

Judi Beker

On a muggy July day in 1941 in Kovno, Lithuania, 12-year-old Judi Beker stood in the courtyard of her home, quivering in anguish. German soldiers had just ordered Judi and her entire family—mother Mina, brother Abe, 14, and sister Rachel, 16—out of their house forever with hardly a moment's notice.

The Bekers had already gathered whatever they could carry, but when Mina didn't move fast enough to suit the Germans, a soldier yanked her out of the house by her hair.

"Let's go! Move! Move! Faster! Faster!" the Germans shouted. They shoved the Bekers down the street, where they joined thousands of other Jews who were being herded into a ghetto in Kovno (today known as Kaunas).

On the way, Judi and her family ducked stones and

sticks hurled by children who, egged on by their parents, cursed at and spit on them. Whatever landed on Judi didn't hurt nearly as much as the heartache she felt. *They are my friends. How could they be so mean?* she wondered. These were the same kids who, during the past few years, played tag and hopscotch and shared jokes and candy with her. These were the same girls who exchanged dolls with her and dressed them in clothes that her own mother had made just for them. *I don't understand.*

"Mother, why are they doing this to us?" Judi whimpered. "Why do they hate us?"

"Because we are Jews," Mina replied.

"But they are my friends."

"Well, now they're not."

As her eyes welled up from the hurt caused by the kids' harsh bigotry, Judi fell in step with a stream of weeping Jews who were clutching their hastily bundled belongings. They plodded across the bridge over the Neris River to the closely guarded, barbed-wire–enclosed ghetto in nearby Slobodka, an area of small primitive houses and no running water.

Nearly 30,000 Jews were packed into the overcrowded ghetto, forcing the Bekers to live with three other families, including one with six children. Many Jews during the war were forced to work as slave laborers for the German war machine, constructing military camps and roads. Others toiled in sweatshops, making clothes and supplies for soldiers.

With deliberate callousness, the Germans rationed the amount of food available to the ghetto, creating hunger on a massive scale. Each person was allowed only a few ounces of bread per day, two ounces of horse meat every two weeks, and a bag of potatoes once a month. To ease her hunger pangs, Judi sometimes ate grass.

Shortly after their arrival, a Jewish man named Motke asked Judi, "How would you like to help feed your family and others, too?"

"Sure," she replied. "What do I have to do?"

"Get food from the black market. I'm organizing children who don't look Jewish—who have blond hair and blue eyes like you—to sneak out of the ghetto and smuggle food back in. I won't lie to you. It could be dangerous."

"I'll do it," said Judi.

Most nights over the next several weeks, Judi collected jewelry and other small valuables from ghetto inhabitants. She then crawled through an opening in the barbed wire that Motke had made with his pliers. On his instructions, Judi entered certain shops in the "free" areas of the city and traded the valuables for bread, potatoes, and other staples. Food was so scarce that it became outrageously expensive. A diamond ring could buy only five loaves of bread. Because Judi couldn't conceal five loaves on her at one time, she usually hid one under her dress and wrapped the rest in newspaper or burlap and buried them. She returned later to dig up the loaves.

Judi, who hid food in her underwear, tried not to think about the consequences if she was caught by the Germans or other guards. Survival for her and others depended on her ability to bring food into the ghetto.

One time while smuggling a loaf of bread under her arm, Judi was confronted by a policeman who worked for the Nazis. "Lift up your arm," he commanded.

Thinking fast, she lied, "I can't. I hurt it when I fell down the stairs."

"Do as I order!" he hissed, and slapped her hard across the face with the back of his hand. The blow staggered Judi, causing the bread to fall out. "Why, you lying pig!" he bellowed. In a fury, the policeman beat her with his fists. As Judi lay on the ground, bloody and bruised, he warned her, "If I catch you trying to smuggle food in here again, I'll kill you."

And he meant it. Judi had already witnessed street executions. She, like everyone else, lived in constant fear. There was no respite from the terror because every day she saw people beaten or shot. Many disappeared after an *Aktion*. Within the first three months of the ghetto's existence, 12,000 Jews had been massacred by Lithuanian volunteers under German command. On October 29, 1941, the Germans staged what became known as the Great *Aktion*, when 9,200 Jews were shot to death in a single day.

When word of the bloodbath reached the ghetto, Mina tried to comfort her children, saying, "At least we're alive."

Judi responded, "Yes, but for how long?"

Although the young girl certainly wanted to live, she mentally prepared herself to die. But there was one fear she couldn't overcome: that all Jews would be annihilated; that not one Jew would be left to tell the world of the horrors inflicted on them.

Judi never knew when or where an *Aktion* would be launched against the ghetto's remaining Jews. The constant dread ratcheted up her anxiety. She jumped every time a motorcycle roared into view, thinking it was the local Gestapo official spearheading a new *Aktion*. She flinched every time a German officer strode toward her, afraid he would whip her. She held her breath every time she reached a corner, wondering what kind of Nazi evil lurked on the other side.

Whenever the Bekers were ordered to assemble so the Nazis could select Jews for deportation or death, Mina reminded her children to spread out from one another. If the Germans saw a whole family together, they deliberately took only one or two members so those left behind would grieve and lose their will to live.

Through incredible luck, neither Judi nor her family members were among the thousands of Jews who had been loaded aboard trains and taken away. Nor had the Beker children been snared by police hunting at night for young people who didn't hold jobs. The unfortunate ones were caught and disappeared for good.

Afraid that her children might be next, Mina got them slave-labor jobs in late 1942 in the factory where they made boots for the *Wehrmacht*, Germany's regular army. Although it was grueling work for Judi, Rachel, Abe, and their mother, they were together for now and had a job that offered some protection—as small and fragile as it was—from any new *Aktion*.

At 5:30 A.M. by the ghetto's front entrance, all workers stood at attention, no matter what the weather, for *Appell* (roll call). Then, under armed guard, they were made to trot in the predawn darkness for nearly an hour to the factory where they were given a little piece of bread and watered-down soup before they started work.

Judi, whose job was putting the heels on boots, wished she owned a pair to replace her worn-out, torn shoes. *If only I could steal some boots*, she thought. But she nixed the idea after someone was caught trying to swipe a pair. As punishment, the thief was executed, and the rest of the laborers had to work while chained to the floor.

The Bekers plugged away in the factory for 18 months until one rainy day in June 1944, when the Nazis ordered the few thousand remaining Jews to assemble in a big field for transportation to Germany. "It is for your own safety," an official explained. "The Soviet army is nearing the Lithuanian border, and we want to spare you the danger of being in the front line of a battle zone."

Many Jews refused to believe him and tried to escape, but they were gunned down. Others hid. The Bekers decided to go even though they worried that the Germans were lying. For two days, they rode in a convoy of trucks and were given nothing to eat or drink. Feeling sorry for them, people along the route tossed food into the passing vehicles. Then the captives were put on a train of cattle cars that arrived in a secluded, wet, forested area east of the city of Danzig (today known as Gdańsk in northern Poland).

They had arrived at the notorious death camp Stutthof.

Guards ordered women and children off the train, but made the men stay on board because they were going on to Dachau — another infamous concentration camp near Munich, Germany. With no time for good-byes, family members wailed in distress as the train carrying the men chugged out of sight. Judi, Rachel, and Mina wept for their beloved Abe, convinced he was heading to his death.

Entering Stutthof's main gate — the so-called Death Gate — Judi gasped at the sight of a towering pile of shoes and eyeglasses. "Mother, what's that?"

"Don't ask questions," Mina answered, rattled by the grim scene. "I don't know."

But the way she replied made Judi think that her mother did know and didn't want to tell her.

The women and children stood in *Appell* while a heavy-set female guard stomped between the rows, randomly thwacking people with a riding crop. "No one comes out of here alive," she snarled. "You are all doomed."

An S.S. officer then "welcomed" the new inmates: "From now on, you are no longer a person, just a number. All your rights have been left outside the gate. Actually, you do have one right and you are free to exercise it at any time — leave through that chimney." He pointed to the smokestack of the crematorium, where the bodies of those who had been killed were being burned.

Each prisoner was given a number, a striped dress, and a pair of wooden clogs to wear. It didn't matter whether the clothes and shoes fit. Rachel told Judi, "You're lucky. You have a left and a right shoe. I have two rights."

Sadistic female guards hit them and swore at them, shoving them into a building where the walls echoed with screams. All the women and girls had their hair cut off. When it was Judi's turn, the guards didn't use a shaver or shears. Instead, they stood on each side of her and took turns ripping out clumps of her curly golden locks. "This will make nice hair for my daughter's doll," said one of the guards.

The Bekers were assigned to a three-tiered bunk in one of the wooden barracks. Mina slept on the bottom, Judi was in the middle, and Rachel had the top.

Most every day, a transport arrived and dumped off hundreds upon hundreds of Jews from other camps, mainly Auschwitz II–Birkenau, to die here. Because of its busy 150-person-capacity gas chamber, Stutthof was playing a role in the Final Solution, the Nazi plan to annihilate the Jewish people.

Judi felt pity for these walking skeletons, their dark eyes vacant, their bony faces blank. *Are they even aware they're going to the gas chamber?* she wondered.

Then there were the public executions. Prisoners who had violated a rule or been accused of sabotage were either shot or hanged on the camp parade grounds. These killings served as chilling warnings to all the other inmates who were forced to watch.

Judi was sickened whenever she saw the camp commandant's kids attend the executions because they applauded after each prisoner was murdered. *Why would a parent want a child to see such a horrible thing?* she wondered. Then she answered her own question. *Of course, so the children will turn into little Nazis.*

Death was a part of life at Stutthof. Judi not only saw death every day, but she smelled it. The smoke belching from the crematorium's chimney shrouded the camp in a revolting stench that kept the birds away.

Like all the inmates, Judi didn't know what the next minute would bring. Would she be chosen for work in the camp factory or death in the gas chamber? Would she be whipped for no reason or get deathly sick from the latest epidemic? Typhus — an often fatal disease spread by lice and rodents and marked by severe headache, high fever, cough, and rash — was rampant in the camp. So was typhoid fever, a highly infectious and often fatal intestinal disease caused by contaminated water or food.

During *Appell*, no one was allowed to talk, and everyone had to stand at attention and keep his or her eyes open. At this time, Judi put herself in a trance. Mentally, she took herself back to the Lithuanian village of Jasvene (pronounced YAS-ven-ah), where she'd enjoyed a happy childhood for the first nine years of her life.

In her daydream, she envisioned the nasturtiums — brightly colored flowers of red, yellow, and orange — that blossomed around her home. She imagined inhaling the flowers' fragrant aroma. And she imagined smelling fresh-out-of-the-oven challah (a braided bread) that her mother baked every Friday morning for the Sabbath. Each imaginary scent made Judi feel as if she were taking an extra breath of life.

Then Judi heard in her mind the most pleasant sound of all: her mother's sweet voice singing a lullaby to her.

Judi also pictured her father, Osser, a lumber and cattle merchant, who was deeply religious; her relatives who lived in and around Jasvene; and her house, where she and her siblings were schooled by Mina. Judi tried to imagine the secure feeling that once enveloped her — before all the bad things happened: before her father suffered a fatal heart attack in 1938, before war broke out in 1939, before the family moved to Kovno so Mina could find work, before the Germans invaded Lithuania in 1941, before the ghetto and the brutality and the hunger and the murders.

Something, usually the barking orders of a guard, would snap Judi out of her trance and back to the reality of the Stutthof death camp.

"We will survive," Mina always reminded her two daughters. "Remember where you lived before the ghetto — 20 Luksas Gatve. That's where we will meet one day."

Survival here required luck and stamina. Victims not selected for the gas chamber were often worked to death or starved to death. Like other inmates, Judi was wasting away, given only a daily bowl of brown soup with a few peelings of potato or another vegetable. She was constantly thirsty because only one water faucet—opened for one hour a day in the morning and one hour in the evening—served more than 1,500 inmates.

The Bekers often worked in the camp factory, knitting scarves, mittens, and sweaters for the army. The slave laborers put in tweve-hour days, six days a week and half a day on Sunday. It wasn't unusual for Judi to see five or six inmates a day topple off their chairs and die from exhaustion, disease, or hunger.

She and her fellow prisoners shared their barracks with lice, rats, cockroaches, and disease. At night, Judi and Rachel would pinch each other to make sure the other was still alive. In the morning, the bodies of those who died in their sleep were stacked outside the barracks.

Occasionally, the prisoners saw Allied planes fly overhead on bombing missions. "They never attack Stutthof," Rachel complained to her sister. "I pray they'll bomb this place even if it means I'll die."

"I have a different prayer," said Judi. "I pray that if I live, I will never, ever think like a Nazi and that I will always feel for other human beings. Most of all, I pray that I will survive as a Jew."

In the fall, Judi joined a work group that picked potatoes and other vegetables from the camp's large field. As hungry as she was, she didn't dare sneak a bite from a raw vegetable. She saw what happened to inmates who did. They were shot.

Around this time, the camp was ravaged by a typhus epidemic. The disease struck Rachel hard, so Mina and Judi brought her to the infirmary, where the nurses did little but keep her comfortable. Usually, prisoners who went in there died there.

A few days later, during *Appell*, the guards selected Mina and several other women and told them, "Come with us."

"Mama, where are you going?" Judi asked.

"I don't know. I guess to work somewhere."

"I want to go with you."

Mina nodded and motioned for Judi to follow her. They walked past the barracks, past the infirmary, and headed directly toward an ominous concrete building. Judi gasped, stopped in her tracks, and yanked on her mother's arm. "Mama, it's the gas chamber!" Fear had such a stranglehold on Judi's throat that she could barely get out the words.

Mina flinched and struggled to maintain her composure. "It's our turn to die," she said in a wavering voice. "I always thought we would survive. I really did."

A guard hollered, "Take off all your clothes and then line up!"

After the women did what they were told, they stood shivering and crying. Judi stared at the corpses from the previous group that were being carried out of the gas chamber and taken to the crematorium. She didn't regret going to the gas chamber with her mother. *I had no choice*, she told herself. *I had to be with her. She was my only protection. I have no one else. Rachel is in the hospital and might die there. Mama is the only connection I have to my life. Everything else has been taken from me. No matter what, I've always been with her. And now I'm going to die with her.*

Judi clutched her mother's hand as the line moved forward. She stepped closer to the gas chamber door. *I hope it's not painful.*

Closer. *I'll just close my eyes and fall asleep.*

Now they were at the entrance. She squeezed her mother's hand. *I hope death comes quickly.*

Unexpectedly, the guard at the doorway, who was drinking a bottle of beer, glowered at Judi and roared, "Out, you pig, you dog!"

Judi froze, not sure what he was saying or why. Mina let go of her hand, shoved her out of line, and shouted, "Run, Judi! Run!"

The girl dashed naked across an open area, sure that a guard in one of the towers would spot her and shoot her. She sprinted to a bushy area where five female inmates were sorting the dresses of women who had been executed. As soon as Judi crouched next to them, they threw a dress on her and told her, "Hurry to your barrack and pretend you were never here."

When she returned to her quarters, she flopped on her bunk and went into emotional shock. Once she comprehended what had happened — how she escaped a death that claimed her mama — Judi ran to the infirmary and sobbed to her ill sister, "We don't have a mother anymore."

Rachel recovered from typhus but remained weak. The disease, which was claiming about 100 victims a day, struck Judi, too, in early January 1945, but she didn't go to the infirmary.

While dealing with her illness, she walked by a barbed-wire fence that separated the male prisoners from the females. A man wrapped a piece of paper around a rock and hurled it over the fence. Curious, Judi went over and picked it up. Scrawled on the paper was the message: "Hold on. The war will be over soon."

Oh, how I hope that's true, she thought, smiling at the inmate. Unexpectedly, he motioned for her to turn around. She did and gulped. The camp commandant, his face masked in rage, was marching straight toward her. *If he sees me with this message, we'll all be in trouble, especially me.* She turned her back to him, bent over, stuffed the paper in her mouth, and swallowed it.

Angrily waving his lit cigar in front of her face, he demanded, "Where's that paper?"

"I ate it. I was hungry."

Without another word, the commandant struck Judi in the head and torso with his fists. When she tumbled to the snowy ground, he kicked her in the sides and back. Everyone was ordered to return to his or her barrack, leaving the battered girl lying alone in the snow.

After the commandant left the area, Rachel scampered out, picked Judi up, and brought her back inside. It took days for Judi to recover.

Rumors spread throughout the camp that the Soviet army was advancing. Hearing the distant thunder of bombs and artillery, Judi told Rachel, "It sounds like the Russians are getting closer every day. Let's hope they liberate us soon."

Before daybreak on the bitterly cold morning of January 25, the camp's loudspeakers blared, "Get ready! Get ready! In one hour you will leave Stutthof."

"Did you hear that, Rachel?" Judi said. "We're finally getting out of here!"

Under the camp lights, she saw guards hustling from one building to another, cleaning out file cabinets and burning documents. With no coats to keep them warm against the frigid temperatures and howling wind, the sisters wrapped each other in burlap and stuffed paper in their wooden shoes.

An hour later at *Appell*, each of the thousands of prisoners was given a loaf of bread. "Where are the trucks and trains that will take us out of here?" Judi asked her sister.

"There aren't any," Rachel replied. "They're going to make us walk. Judi, they're taking us on a death march!"

In nine lengthy columns under heavy guard, the prisoners were marched out of Stutthof into a ferocious blizzard. Tromping through 15 inches of snow and a fierce headwind was difficult for everyone. Those who staggered out of step were beaten. Those who fell down and couldn't get up were shot.

Hour after hour, the prisoners slogged against the shrieking wind and blinding snow. The extreme cold froze

Judi's nostrils, stung her bare skin, and hurt her teeth when-ever she grimaced.

"Judi, I don't think I can make it much farther," said Rachel. "I'm too weak, too cold."

"I am, too, but we have to keep going." Judi slipped her arm into her sister's and said, "Just stay in step with me, Rachel. One-two, one-two. Walk, walk. We're going to live! Believe me. We're going to live!"

As the afternoon grew darker, Judi thought she heard, in the howling wind, the droning sounds of airplanes. All of a sudden, the ground shook in a fiery explosion off to the left. Then another blast erupted to the right and another and another. Prisoners screamed and ran every which way. Some guards dove for cover; others began shooting at those who were fleeing.

"We're getting bombed!" Judi yelled.

Holding hands, the sisters leaped into a ditch. They wrapped their arms around each other and prayed they wouldn't get blown up. *This is not how I want to die,* Judi thought.

When the attack ended, the guards rounded up the prisoners and ordered them to continue their march of misery. The sisters, however, remained hidden in the ditch until they felt sure that the guards weren't still looking for them.

"Where should we go?" Judi asked.

Pointing to a light in a farmhouse on the far side of a snow-whipped field, Rachel said, "Let's try that place."

As they made their way across the field, they stumbled and fell in the deep snow. To their great relief, they were welcomed inside by two Polish women and a Russian prisoner of war who was working on their farm. The women made the sisters throw away their prison dresses and gave them each a skirt and sweater. Then they wrapped the sisters in blankets and sat them by the fire to thaw out. The women prepared a hot meal, which Judi and Rachel tried to eat, but their shrunken stomachs from months of malnutrition and starvation couldn't handle the food.

Because Rachel could speak Russian, she talked with the POW. He told her, "Those bombs came from Soviet planes. It was probably a mistake. It was getting dark, and the pilots mistook the death march for a German troop movement. You're lucky you're alive and that you came to this house. But you can't stay here. The guards from Stutthof will be searching for escapees."

"Where will we go?" Rachel asked.

"There's a convent on the other side of the Vistula River. You need to get there and stay with the nuns. Tell them you're Catholic. But first change your names to something that doesn't sound Jewish."

"How will we get across the river?"

"It's frozen. You'll crawl to the other side."

After thanking their hosts, Judi and Rachel left with the Russian. After leading them through fields and woods to a spot where the wide river was at its narrowest, he bade them good luck and left.

In the dead of night, Judi and Rachel slowly crawled across the ice. Early the next morning, they reached the convent and told the nuns they were orphaned Lithuanians running for their lives from the fighting between the Germans and Russians. Their only lie: Judi said her name was Utta and Rachel gave her name as Anna. They failed to mention they were Jewish.

But the nuns, who gave them a warm welcome, knew. "Utta" and "Anna" were skin and bones, sick, and covered with sores—familiar traits of Jewish prisoners. The local radio station had already broadcast an alert that several inmates from Stutthof had escaped, and urged listeners to turn them in.

The nuns bathed the girls—their first hot bath in four years—and fed them soothing porridge and other simple fare because of the condition of their stomachs. Both girls were given clean underwear and new clothes, including a scarf so Judi could cover the sores on her bald head.

Over the next two weeks, the girls did easy chores around the convent while trying to regain their strength. Meanwhile, radio broadcasts announced a reward for turning in escaped Jews, so the girls felt they had to stay in the convent. Besides, Judi was getting sicker from typhus.

But they were faced with a dilemma when a nun told the girls, "We know you're Jewish. For your own survival, you must be baptized Catholics."

"But why?" asked Judi.

"If the authorities find you hiding here, they'll take you away and kill you and punish us. But if you're Catholic, they'll leave you and us alone. You can stay here as long as you want or until you're well enough to return home."

Neither Judi nor Rachel wanted to convert. That evening in their room, Judi shared her feelings with her big sister. "We might be the only two Jews still alive," she said. "I want to stay a Jew."

Rachel agreed. "We were brought up Jewish, and it's important that we survive as Jews."

"I have nothing against their religion. But if it's a choice between living as a Catholic or dying as a Jew, I'd rather die a Jew."

"Then it's settled," said Rachel. "We're sneaking out of here tonight."

Before leaving through their first-floor bedroom window, Judi snatched two rosaries. "We might need them to help convince people we're Catholic," she explained.

As they clomped in the snow away from the convent, Judi said, "I feel bad that we didn't say good-bye and thank the nuns for all they did. They were so kind to us."

"The only way we'll get a chance to thank them later is if we survive."

The girls walked west toward Danzig hoping to find food, shelter, and work. But the most pressing need was for Judi to get medical attention. When they reached Danzig, Rachel brought Judi to a hospital and told her, "You stay here and get well. I'll come back for you once I find a job and a place for us to stay."

Judi received the necessary treatment until she was strong enough to leave the hospital. "Did you find us room and board?" she asked Rachel.

"Yes, but it could be risky. We'll be working for a woman who runs a Wehrmacht duty station. It's a place where the German soldiers get their ammunition and sleep overnight and eat."

"Are you crazy, Rachel?"

"It's all that I could find. There's more to tell you. Her name is Mrs. Arenstein, and she's not pleasant at all. She has a bunch of children, and her husband is an S.S. officer."

"Can it get any worse?"

"We have to pretend to be Catholic and attend Mass with her."

After Rachel introduced Judi to Mrs. Arenstein, the woman gave the girls a few hand-me-down clothes. Then she turned abusive. She ordered them around like slaves and sometimes beat them while they worked. She made them sleep in the barn, gave them little food, and refused to pay them, claiming room and board was payment enough. "It's like slave labor all over again," Judi whined to Rachel.

"Maybe we should leave and find work elsewhere."

"I have no energy," said Judi, who was still suffering the effects of typhus. "We have to stay here until I get stronger."

Mrs. Arenstein's cruelty knew no bounds. After her children ate dinner, she put the leftovers in a bowl on the floor.

Then she tied Judi's and Rachel's hands behind their backs and forced them to get on their knees and eat like dogs. If the girls' eating didn't amuse her children, she pressed a pitchfork in the sisters' backs.

But on Sundays, she acted like a different person. She gave the sisters better clothes to wear and took them to Mass. She treated them nicely—but only in front of other people at church. When the girls returned to the Wehrmacht duty station, she reverted to her nasty self.

One day while the sisters were serving dinner to German troops, a soldier asked Mrs. Arenstein, "Those girls are really skinny. Are they from a concentration camp?"

"No," she replied. "They're my slaves. I let them sleep in the barn with the animals. They're nothing. They're Lithuanian."

"Oh, that's funny because we just came from Lithuania. We burned down the entire ghetto in Kovno. There are no more Jews left."

"I'll drink to that!" shouted one of the soldiers at the table. All the Germans in the dining room held up their beer and began singing.

Once the sisters left the room, Judi began to cry. "Did you hear what he said, Rachel? There are no more Jews. We're the only ones left."

With each passing week, Allied bombing of the area and aerial dogfights intensified. About a month after the girls had arrived at the Wehrmacht duty station, Judi was chopping wood out back when she heard someone moaning in the forest. She went to investigate and found a wounded German pilot who had parachuted out of a crippled plane. Even though he was the enemy, she didn't pretend to ignore him or try to hurt him.

Without hesitating, she took her apron off, tied it around him, and dragged him toward the station. A warm feeling flowed through her. *I can still feel for another person. There's still some humanity left in me.*

When Rachel saw Judi lugging the wounded pilot, she glowered at her and said, "Are you nuts? He's a German. He's probably killed many Jews."

"But he's a human being."

Suddenly, bombs started falling near the station. People left their homes and the station and raced to the air-raid shelter. Someone motioned to the girls to hurry up, but Rachel and Judi remained with the wounded German. Seconds later, a bomb blew up the air-raid shelter, killing many inside.

The girls held each other and jumped up and down. "Thank God, we're alive!" Rachel shouted. "If you hadn't helped that German pilot, we would have been in that shelter."

The following day, Mrs. Arenstein, who wasn't injured in the attack, told the sisters, "We can't stay here any longer. Everyone is evacuating the area, so you're going with me to Denmark. It's safer there because it's still under German control."

They boarded a small freighter crammed with soldiers and Nazi sympathizers. While the sisters stood in the middle of the crowded deck, the ship cleared the harbor. Without warning, a violent explosion ripped into the hull. "We've been torpedoed!" someone shouted.

Smoke billowed up from below, and flames began to spread. As passengers screamed in panic, the vessel listed badly, pitching Judi and Rachel into the bone-chilling Baltic Sea. "I can't swim!" Judi cried.

She thrashed her way in the water before latching on to a floating plank. Rachel managed to reach it, too. "We're still alive," she said through chattering teeth. Together they clung to the plank, praying that they would be rescued before the numbing cold sapped the life out of them.

The girls were nearly unconscious when sailors from a passing boat plucked them from the icy water, wrapped them in blankets, and took them to Copenhagen, Denmark, about 300 miles away.

The sisters were placed in a gymnasium for refugees and given basic medical care. Judi, now 16, weighed just 47 pounds. When she looked in a mirror, she nearly collapsed. *I hardly recognize myself.* Doctors told her she would need extensive hospitalization and outpatient care. For months, she got around in a wheelchair.

On May 5, 1945—two months after the girls landed in Copenhagen—Denmark was liberated. Officials in the refugee gymnasium announced that if there were any Jews in the building, they must report to the Red Cross desk. "I'm afraid to tell them I'm Jewish," Judi told Rachel. "What if it's a hoax? If they know we're Jews, they might kill us."

"No, Judi, the war is over. We have to do this because we might be the only Jews left."

When they approached a woman from the Danish Red Cross, Judi asked, "Are there any other Jews?"

"Most definitely," the woman replied. "In a couple of weeks, thousands of Danish Jews will return."

Rachel asked, "How do you know?"

"Because we helped them escape." The woman explained that although Denmark had been occupied by the German army since 1940, the Danes secretly pulled off one of the greatest humanitarian efforts of the war. Under the noses of the Nazis, the Danes hid 8,000 of their Jewish neighbors in their homes and then sneaked them aboard hundreds of private fishing boats that spirited them to safety in nearby Sweden, a neutral country.

The Beker sisters were dumbfounded. "Imagine, we've come to a place where they risked their lives to save Jews," Judi said. "The Danes see Jews as friends and neighbors, not as people to hate."

"They're starting to restore my faith in humankind," said Rachel.

The girls were at the dock when the first big ship carrying returning Jews arrived from Sweden. The pier erupted in cheers, laughter, and sobs of joy. From her wheelchair, Judi soaked in the magical scene and marveled, "Look, Rachel. They're Jews who survived just like us. Isn't it wonderful? The Jewish people live!"

Judi, who suffered many health problems, was in and out of the hospital for two and a half years in Copenhagen. Helping her recover was a childless Lutheran couple, Sven and Paula Jensen, who cared for her and Rachel in Denmark for four years.

During that time, the truth of the atrocities inflicted on the Jews came to light. It was learned that in 1941, about 650 Jews in Judi's hometown of Jasvene and the surrounding area were marched by the Einsatzgruppen—Nazi killing squads—to a remote field near Ariogala, Lithuania, where they were executed and dumped into a mass grave. Among the dead were 146 of her relatives, including 43 children.

Also, an estimated 85,000 people died over the years at Stutthof before it was evacuated. On the death march in January 1945, from which the Beker sisters escaped, about 5,000 prisoners were marched to the coast of the Baltic Sea, forced into the water, and machine-gunned.

Of the 30,000 Jews ordered into the Kovno ghetto—where Judi, Rachel, and Mina lived for three years—only 2,000 survived the war.

As for Mrs. Arenstein, she was arrested in Copenhagen and deported after Judi and Rachel testified against her.

In 1946, the Beker sisters got the surprise of their lives—a postcard from their brother, Abe, whom they assumed was dead. He had survived the horrors of Dachau and was living in Toronto, Canada.

Wanting to be with her brother, Judi immigrated to Canada in 1949 and, a year later, married Gabe Cohen, whom she met on the voyage over. Rachel, who had wed a Dane, also immigrated to Canada. In 1952, Judi and Gabe moved to Philadelphia where they raised three children while she earned a degree in early childhood development at Temple University.

Judi became an activist in 1963, after an African-American family moved into an all-white neighborhood in a Philadelphia suburb. Seeing a news report of a hate-filled mob of white people harassing the family, Judi felt devastated because the scene reminded her of the vicious bigotry that had ignited the Holocaust.

Up to this point, she had seldom mentioned the Holocaust to her children because she didn't want to traumatize them. But she realized it was her duty to promote tolerance and acceptance by telling others about her life of persecution, so she began giving speeches throughout the country. Deeply involved in the civil rights movement, Judi participated in and helped organize the March on Washington in 1963, where Dr. Martin Luther King delivered his famous "I Have a Dream" speech in front of 250,000 marchers.

Today she goes by the name of Judith Meisel. Married to her second husband, Fred Meisel, she lives in Santa Barbara, California, and continues to speak at high schools, churches, colleges, and teacher-training seminars. She is the focus of a documentary (available in DVD) about her life, called Tak for Alt, Danish for "thanks for everything."

"Never in my life under Nazi persecution did I dream I would one day have three children and seven grandchildren," says Judith. "When I held my first grandchild, Aaron, I held him for the one and a half million children who died in the Holocaust. Had they survived, they would have been grandparents like me.

"Some people ask if I ever wanted revenge for all the horror and terror that I suffered. Well, I have my revenge. I survived. What I went through during the Holocaust empowered me do something to try to make the world a better place."

"We Must Find a Way to Escape from Here!"

≡

Halina Litman

By her ninth birthday, Halina Litman clearly understood what her Jewish faith meant to the German occupiers of her town: death.

Before the war, her hometown of Zaleszczyki (pronounced zal-ish-CHICK-ee), a Polish resort of 5,000 people, was a delightful place to grow up. Red and white cherry trees lined the main road, and elegantly trimmed trees shaded the paved streets. The markets overflowed with locally grown peaches, apricots, melons, and grapes. Nestled on a peninsula, the town was surrounded on three sides by the wide, swift-flowing Dniester River. Every summer, tourists flocked to its sandy beaches to swim and sunbathe. Colorful kayaks darted along the river while loudspeakers from beachside restaurants played classical and dance music throughout the day and into the evening.

In the summer, Halina—called Halinka by her family—swam and kayaked, having developed a love for water from her mother, Olga, who, as a teenager, had been a record-breaking swimming champion for three years. In the winter, Halina skated on the frozen river with her mother and her father, Ignacy, a dentist.

However, life changed quickly and unexpectedly. In September 1939—two months after the birth of Halina's sister, Ewa (pronounced Eva)—Germany invaded Poland from the west, and the Soviet Union took control of the east, fracturing the country in two. When Soviet troops marched into Zaleszczyki, Halina's father panicked and fled into nearby Romania. Ignacy left without his family because he believed that men were in danger, but not women and children. Several weeks later, he changed his mind and tried to return home, but the Russians had sealed the borders. They arrested him, tried him as a spy, and sentenced him to 20 years hard labor in Siberia. Typically, in the Soviet system of justice at the time, if one person was convicted, members of his or her whole family were also sent away. Fortunately, the Litmans had friends who knew people influential with the Soviets and persuaded officials to spare the family from being shipped off to Siberia.

Life was hard for most Jews under the Soviet occupation, but it turned much worse after the German army ousted the Russians in July 1941 and controlled all of Poland, including Zaleszczyki. The Germans immediately began to persecute the Jews, taking over their businesses and kicking some out of their homes. All Jews had to wear yellow stars on their sleeves and paint a yellow star on their homes so the Germans could easily identify them. Failure to do so was an offense punishable by death. When Jews were ordered to turn over their valuables, Olga, like most people, hid some.

On November 14, 1941 — a month shy of Halina's ninth birthday — the Germans conducted their first *Aktion* in Zaleszczyki. Following orders from their occupiers, about 1,000 Jews in the town assembled voluntarily in the main square. Told they would bind young trees with burlap to protect the saplings from the harsh winter, the Jews were taken to an old Polish military camp.

The Litmans remained home. That evening, Halina asked Olga, "*Mamusiu* [Polish for "Mommy," pronounced ma-MOO-shoe], shouldn't all those people have returned home by now? It's awfully dark."

"Yes. They should have been back hours ago."

The next morning when her mother returned from the market, Halina was alarmed by Olga's drawn face and bloodshot eyes. "Mamusiu, have you been crying? What's wrong?"

"Horrendous news," Olga replied, slumping into a kitchen chair. "A girl from the work group showed up at the market and told everyone about an unspeakable massacre. She said when they reached the forest, they began binding trees. The Germans took about two hundred people and sent them to the Kamionka labor camp to work. Then the

Germans took forty others and made them dig a giant hole. When it was finished, the rest of the people were brought to the hole and ordered to stand over it and"—Olga broke down and cried—"the soldiers machine-gunned them. The hole was their mass grave!"

Hearing about the slaughter floored Halina—and terrified her. "No, this can't be true. It must be a lie. I know the Germans hate us, but they wouldn't go and kill innocent people."

"Innocent? In the eyes of those Nazi monsters, we are all guilty—guilty of being Jews."

Still not wanting to believe the atrocity, Halina asked, "How did the girl survive?"

"She started running away, and they shot at her. She tripped and fell, and they assumed they had killed her, but the bullets missed her. When the soldiers left, she got up and rushed back here to warn us. Everyone is petrified and in a state of shock. Halinka, eight hundred innocent Jews from our town were murdered in cold blood!"

Seized with fright, Halina threw her arms around her weeping mother and cried. The girl could feel Olga's body trembling. "Mamusiu, I'm so scared."

"So am I, Halinka. So am I."

When will they come for us? the girl wondered. *There's no place for Jews to go. Poor Mamusiu. She has me and a baby to worry about.*

With a curfew in place and the roads guarded by soldiers, the remaining Jews felt trapped. No one knew when the next *Aktion* would take place in the town, causing everyone to live in fear, even though they continued to carry out their daily tasks.

Helping her mother in the market a few weeks later, Halina spotted a family friend who was a member of the *Judenrat*—a council of Jews hand-picked by the Germans to carry out the orders of the Nazis. The man motioned for Olga to come over. Halina, carrying a basket of fruit and vegetables, followed her mother. The man was nervous. "Olga," he whispered. "There's going to be another *Aktion* tomorrow. Go and find a place for you and your children to hide."

Halina was so scared she dropped her basket, spilling the contents. As she picked them up, her mind was racing. *What are we going to do? Where will we go? How will we escape?*

Later that day, Halina saw her mother gather up the silverware and asked, "What are you going to do with it, Mamusiu?"

"It's our ticket to safety—I hope," Olga replied. She explained that she was giving the silverware to their neighbor Rozia as payment for letting them hide in her house across the street. Rozia, who had been the family's cook before the war, was a Catholic and not a target of the latest *Aktion*.

That day Halina and her mother and little sister hurried across the street to Rozia's home. Seconds after the Litmans stepped inside, the head of the S.S. in the region roared down the street in his motorcycle ahead of his men, looking for anyone wearing yellow armbands. Throughout the day, the sound of gunfire, screams, and shouts filled the air as soldiers burst into the homes of Jews and pulled them out. By morning, thousands of men, women, and children had been hauled off to what the Germans claimed was a work camp. No one ever saw them again.

By the winter of 1941–1942, conditions had worsened considerably. Many Jews died of hunger and typhoid. The following spring and summer brought more misery for Jews, who were randomly shot, beaten, or sent to nearby labor camps.

During this time, a neighbor used bribery to release a relative from a concentration camp. When the released man arrived in the village, Halina was shocked at how gaunt and frail he appeared. "He looks half dead," she told her mother.

"Those Germans are so wicked," Olga said. "First they take away everything he has, and then they make his family pay to get him out of the camp. You know what will happen next? They will arrest him again and bleed his family dry of all their money. It's the same story for thousands of other Jews."

On September 20, 1942, the Germans expelled Zaleszczyki's remaining Jews and shipped them to the nearby town of Tluste. Most, including the Litmans, were forced to live in a Jewish neighborhood and share a house with several other families. Fearing another *Aktion*, all the

Jews began frantically creating hiding places and digging escape tunnels.

Over the next several weeks, armed Gestapo surrounded the Jewish quarter and dragged people from their homes. Those who were not shot on the spot for resisting or trying to flee were then assembled and crammed onto trains, which carried them away to concentration camps.

When Olga was tipped off about another *Aktion*, she paid two non-Jewish farmers to hide her and the children. She left Halina in the care of a farmer's wife and told the girl, "You stay here with Mrs. Butowski. Ewa and I will be hiding at another farm close by."

"But, Mamusiu . . ."

"Be strong. I'm counting on you. I'll come for you once this *Aktion* is over."

Throughout the day, as Jews were being caught and put under guard in the square, Mrs. Butowski grew more upset. She kept giving Halina, who was hiding in the loft of the house, updates — including a report on the capture of one of Olga's best friends and the woman's infant son. "Her family wanted her to hide with them. But she wouldn't go with them because she was afraid her baby would cry and give away their secret hiding place," Mrs. Butowski told Halina. "And now she's being taken away."

Hearing the news, Halina feared the worst for her mother and three-year-old sister. *I just know they've been captured and I'll never see them again.* Her stomach hurt from anguish.

Hours passed with no word from her mother. Halina was slowly losing hope when, later that evening, Olga showed up with Ewa. "Mamusiu, Ewa, you're safe!" Halina cried, rushing to them.

After hugging them, Halina noticed her mother's face. The girl had never seen her so shaken before. Olga broke down and wept. "It was awful, Halinka. The farmer who was hiding us panicked when she heard soldiers were searching other farms. She threw us out in broad daylight. I ran with Ewa into an open field; it had only one bush. We crouched under it, hoping we wouldn't be discovered. There were Germans all over and planes were flying overhead, and it was a miracle that they didn't see us. At the end of the day, a kind woman who had spotted us but didn't tell anyone brought milk for Ewa. After it turned dark, I left the bush and came here."

"Mamusiu, I don't want to be away from you anymore."

"You won't, Halinka. From now on, whatever happens, we will stick together."

When she learned that the Germans, in the latest *Aktion*, had deported about 1,000 Jews and murdered 200 more, Halina pleaded with her mother, "Mamusiu, we must find a way to escape from here!"

"Yes, Halinka, we'll find a way," Olga promised.

With the help of friends at the *Judenrat*, Olga made contact with a priest who provided new identities for the Litmans. For a price, he created baptismal documents for

Olga, Halina, and Ewa, giving them new identities as Polish Catholics. The papers would allow them to leave Tluste in the hope of escaping the ongoing persecution.

From now on, their last name would be a Polish non-Jewish one — Litynska. Halina's new identity meant she had to learn a new birth date, place of birth, and place of baptism, as well as new names for grandparents and god-parents. She also had to learn basic Catholic rituals such as making the sign of the cross when entering a church.

"You're lucky, Halina," said Olga. "You don't look Jewish, because you have green eyes and blond hair. But we need to put your hair in braids so you look more like a Polish Catholic."

Fiddling with her new braids, Halina gazed into the mirror and told her mother, "Nobody will think I'm Jewish. I know this new appearance will help me survive, but I feel angry that I can't tell people the truth."

"You have to be careful, Halinka," her mother said. "No one must know. No one."

"Don't worry, Mamusiu. I won't tell anyone. I know we must pretend we're not Jewish. It's the only way we'll get out of here."

Armed with their false papers, the Litmans took a train bound for Jaroslaw [pronounced ya-ROS-waf] in southeast-ern Poland. Olga chose the town because she knew a man who lived there, and she was counting on his help. After the train left Tluste, Halina thought, *I never want to see that place again.* Her sense of relief over escaping was tempered by anxiety over what awaited them in Jaroslaw, which, like the rest of Poland, was controlled by the Germans. The Litmans had no real plan other than to get out of Tluste and avoid persecution.

During the incredibly slow train ride to Jaroslaw, which took nearly four days to complete, the trio shared a compartment with a seemingly friendly Polish man in his early thirties. His eyes twinkled when he talked to the girls, and he displayed a pleasant manner and a sympathetic ear. To Halina, he seemed like a nice man. But he kept coaxing and pressing Olga to talk more openly about her heritage.

On the third day of the trip, he said, "You can be honest with me, Mrs. Litynska. Do you have any Jewish blood in you? Was your father or mother Jewish?"

Like so many times before Olga, denied it. But having been under enormous strain throughout the trip, she finally cracked under his constant pressure. She sighed and admitted, "Yes, I am Jewish. We all are."

The man put his hands together and smiled. "Ah, I thought so."

Hearing her mother reveal the truth to this stranger—no matter how nice he seemed—frightened Halina. *But I thought we were never to say we're Jewish.*

"Are you Jewish, too?" Olga asked him.

"No, my dear Mrs. Litynska, or whoever you really are. I'm a *Volksdeutsche*."

Olga recoiled in horror. She threw her hands up to her face and gasped. "Oh, no!" She burst into sobs.

Perplexed and petrified, Halina asked, "Mamusiu, what's wrong? What's a *Volksdeutsche*?"

Olga couldn't speak and kept crying, so the man answered, "A *Volksdeutsche* is a Polish citizen of German ancestry who fully supports the Nazi Party."

"You mean you're not our friend?"

"Well, I'll look after you for the rest of the trip." He directed his gaze at Olga and said, "You understand that once we arrive at our destination, it's my duty, my obligation as a *Volksdeutsche,* to turn in the three of you to the Gestapo."

"Yes, I know," Olga blubbered, still sick about revealing her true identity. When she regained her composure, she said, "I want to make a deal with you. I'll give you my money and all our possessions if you will promise me that when we get to the Gestapo station, we will all be shot immediately. I can't bear the thought of being separated from my children and seeing them suffer at the hands of the Gestapo."

"I think that can be arranged." He held out his hand and insisted that Olga shake it. "Now then," he said gaily, "let me get you and the girls a little treat."

Halina couldn't believe her ears. *He's taking us to the Gestapo so they can kill us?* She was scared stiff, unable to move a muscle. *How are we ever going to escape?*

When the train arrived at the station, he politely helped them onto the railroad platform. "Come with me," he said. "I don't want any trouble."

Halina thought, *No! No! No! This can't be happening to us!* Tugging on her mother's skirt, the girl blurted, "Mamusiu, I don't want to die! Please, don't let him do this to us." She faced the man and repeated, "I don't want to die!"

Her eyes clouded with tears, Olga turned to the man and said, "Please let my daughter go. She doesn't look Jewish at all. Maybe she can survive on her own."

"No, no, Mamusiu," Halina cried. "I don't want to leave you. I don't want to be left alone. I want to be with you and Ewa. I want us to get away from this evil man."

"And go where?" Olga said with a sigh.

Halina saw in her mother's weary eyes that she had given up. Facing the man, the girl pleaded, "Don't have us shot. Please!"

The man was unmoved. "I'm sorry. But it's my duty. Keep walking."

As they headed out of the train station toward Gestapo headquarters, Halina wanted to bolt free, but she couldn't bring herself to leave her mother and baby sister. "How can you do this to us?" she told the man. "I'm ten years old and Ewa is only three."

Olga then asked him, "Do you have any children of your own?"

The man stopped walking and nodded. His expression softened.

"Do you really want the deaths of three innocent people on your conscience?" Olga asked him. "Look, I've given you everything I have. Just let us go and we'll try our luck."

He remained still and pondered what Olga and Halina had said to him.

What's he going to do? "Please let us go," Halina begged. "Please."

Finally, he threw his hands up in the air and growled, "Okay, I'll let you go. You don't stand a chance of surviving here, anyway."

The tension that had been building in Halina's body began melting away.

"Here, you'll need this," he said, handing Olga some of the money she had given him. "Get the girls something to eat." Then he spun on his heels and disappeared into the crowd, leaving the relieved Litmans standing in the middle of the street.

Halina hugged her mother and said, "I'm so happy we got rid of him."

"Yes, what a relief. But we're in a strange town with nowhere to go. He took most of our money and all our luggage tickets."

"Right now I don't care," said Halina. "I'm so happy because we still have each other."

They entered a café and got something to drink. Upon learning they needed a place to stay, a patron led them to the bungalow of Mrs. Peszke, a warmhearted Catholic washerwoman who accepted lodgers. To pay for room and board, Olga got a job as a maid in the town while Halina helped Mrs. Peszke with household chores and looked after Ewa, who was frail and sickly. In their tiny room off the kitchen, the Litmans slept in one bed, Olga and the toddler at the head and Halina curled up at the foot.

Halina figured that their life would improve once her mother visited the family friend who was living in Jaroslaw. But when Olga returned after seeing him, Halina saw that she was disheartened. "What's wrong, Mamusiu?"

"He panicked when he saw me," Olga replied. "There aren't supposed to be any Jews left in Jaroslaw, and he's afraid that he will be arrested if he's seen with me. He gave me some money and told me, 'Don't ever come back here again.'"

Often at the dinner table, Halina heard the ugly words of anti-Semitism coming out of the mouths of the other boarders. She knew not to say anything to them.

When Olga went to work, Halina attended school for two hours a day, one of which was spent studying the Catholic religion. Rather than slink into a desk in the back of the room, she sat in the front row to give the priest the impression she was a good Catholic. She learned the Hail Mary and the Our Father. She looked forward to Sundays when the family attended Mass, because people were more relaxed and she liked the smell of incense that the priests used in the ceremony.

One time she came out of church and, after dipping her finger in holy water, crossed herself with her left hand rather than doing it correctly with her right. She was afraid that someone had noticed her miscue, figured out she was a fake Catholic, and would report her to the Gestapo. Fortunately, no one did.

"Mrs. Peszke wants to save my soul," Halina told her mother. "I think she suspects that we're not who we say we are. She wants to send me to special catechism classes so I can receive communion."

"I think it's a good idea that you do as she suggests," Olga said.

"Does that mean I have to get baptized first?"

"No. The fake identity papers claim you already have been baptized."

"I'm not going to tell anyone I'm Jewish, but I sure wish I could. I still don't understand why the Nazis want to kill us just because of our religion."

"The world has gone mad, Halinka."

Halina attended special classes and received communion, much to Mrs. Peszke's satisfaction. No one knew the Litmans were Jewish—not even Ewa, who was too young to understand. The bond between Halina and Olga over their shared secret strengthened with each passing month. "Any little mistake—the slightest thing—could end up costing us our lives," Olga warned her. "Life is so cheap. The Nazis are always looking for Jews to kill."

Fearful of having her Jewish identity discovered, Olga shaved Ewa's hair so people wouldn't notice that the toddler had curly dark locks—a typical Jewish trait.

To minimize the chances of being arrested, Olga told Halina of a bold plan: "The safest place for me to hide is in plain sight. I'm going to apply for a job at the German military camp."

"Why would you do that, Mamusiu?"

"The Germans like having people work for them. If I can get an official military ID card, I can show it if we are ever challenged. That can be a big help."

Trying to mask her nervousness, Olga applied for a job at the base. She was told that her documents had to be checked before she could be hired. For several weeks, she and Halina lived in fear that the Germans would discover her documents were fake. But the papers passed examination, and she was hired to work in the base's kitchen. The job had its perks because Olga was able to steal small amounts of food to bring back to her children.

Halina did her part to find food. After school, she and her friends would sneak into the orchards and steal fruit off the trees. They also would run after farmers' wagons, quietly jump on the back, and swipe some of the produce that the farmers were required to deliver to the Germans.

After coming home from school one day, Halina found her mother flashing a wide smile. Olga announced, "Your father is alive!"

"Oh, how wonderful!" Halina shouted. "How do you know? Where is he?"

"He's safe in Palestine. He sent a letter through the Red Cross to our old home in Zaleszczyki saying he was alive and well." She explained that one of their former neighbors had accepted the letter and given it to the person who helped the Litmans get out of Tluste. In his letter, Ignacy said he had escaped from prison and joined a Polish army unit that had been formed in Russia, which was now on the side of the Allies. He was stationed in Egypt and was able to visit his sister in Palestine (known today as Israel), where she had immigrated years earlier.

"Can we write to him?" Halina asked.

"Unfortunately, there's no way we can communicate with the outside world right now," Olga replied. "We have to wait until the war is over, and then we will find him so he can get us out of Poland."

"I wish this war would hurry up and end."

On a bright morning in July 1944, Halina woke up and noticed something strange. It was deathly silent outside. No birds chirping. No cart-pulling horses clomping. No soldiers marching. She couldn't understand why, so she got out of bed and gazed out the window. Ewa was sleeping, but Olga was awake although still lying in bed. "Mamusiu, it seems too quiet. I wonder—"

KA-BOOM!

A thunderous explosion tore through the house with such force that the roof caved in over the kitchen, spraying their room with dust and debris. Knocked to the floor, Halina screamed and instantly felt a piercing pain in her left hand. When she examined it, she shrieked even louder. A piece of shrapnel had sliced into her hand, splitting open her palm and some of her fingers. Her thumb was hanging by a piece of skin and half of her little finger was gone.

"My hand! My hand!" Halina cried. Olga leaped out of bed, grabbed Ewa, and shouted, "Halina, come with me!"

They scrambled out of the room, climbed over the rubble from the collapsed roof, and ran outside. Not seeing anyone who could help them, they hurried to the hospital a few blocks away.

"What happened?" the dazed girl asked. "Why did the house blow up?"

Because they didn't have access to any news, Halina and Olga weren't aware of any developments in the war. They had no idea that the Germans had retreated when Soviet forces closed in on the area. The Litmans didn't realize that a bomb from a plane had missed its mark and fallen directly on the house, demolishing it.

After Halina arrived at the hospital, nurses cleaned the wound as best they could and told Olga, "We'll probably have to amputate her hand. We have no penicillin to prevent infections."

Halina just wanted the pain to go away, so if it meant cutting off her hand, she could live with that. Seeing a look of devastation on her mother's face, Halina said, "It'll be all right, Mamusiu."

"No, it won't," Olga fretted. "You'll be scarred for life."

She's worried that nobody will want to marry someone with a damaged hand, Halina thought. "That's all right, Mamusiu. So I won't get married. At least I'm alive. We all are."

Hoping for the best, the nurses did not amputate but instead bandaged her up and admitted her to the hospital. Olga and Ewa stayed with Halina for the first few nights before a neighbor, Mrs. Cieplicka, took the two of them in.

When Olga returned to the hospital, she told Halina, "I have some awful news: Mrs. Peszke is dead. She was killed in the explosion."

Halina burst into tears. "She was so kind to us, Mamusiu. She didn't deserve to die."

"None of the innocent ever do."

Halina remained in the hospital for weeks as the medical staff, hampered by a lack of supplies, worked to save her injured hand.

"Is the war over yet?" she asked during one of her mother's frequent visits to the hospital.

Olga shook her head and said, "They're still fighting in other parts of Poland. Just because the Russians are here doesn't mean we're safe. A lot of hatred still exists toward the Jews. At dinner last night, Mrs. Cieplicka's son said, 'Too bad the Germans didn't finish the job and kill all the Jews.' It's very dangerous here. Halinka, you must continue to hide your Jewish identity."

"But I want to tell everyone who I am. I'm tired of living a lie."

"You can't tell anyone. Our lives depend on it. Some of the Jews who came out from hiding, thinking it was safe because the Germans are gone, were murdered by Polish anti-Semites. You have to keep pretending."

"What about Ewa? She's five years old and isn't afraid to talk to adults. What if she says something?"

"Ewa doesn't even know she's Jewish. It hurts me because she's starting to believe the awful things that anti-Semites say. We were at a shop and someone said to her, 'Now you can tell us. You're Jewish, right?' And Ewa said to him, 'Look at me. Do I have horns? Do I have a tail? Of course, I'm not Jewish.'"

Halina winced and felt her mother's heartache.

Two months after the bomb had dropped on Mrs. Peszke's home, Halina left the hospital with her left hand intact minus a thumb and half a little finger.

As the war wound down, Olga sent a letter to a radio station in Palestine. She asked the station to broadcast an announcement that the family of Ignacy Litman wanted him to contact them. In a remarkable stroke of good luck, a woman at the radio station knew him personally and gave him the address of his family.

When the war ended and the family was reunited, Halina no longer had to lie about her religious heritage. "I'm Jewish," she said proudly to those who asked. Being Jewish no longer meant possible death for her. It meant renewed life.

═══

Virtually all the Jews of Halina's hometown of Zaleszczyki were either killed or deported. Few survivors returned after the war. The town is now part of the neighboring country of Ukraine and is spelled Zalishchyky.

Halina and her family reunited with her father, and they immigrated to England in 1947. As a way of coping with her shyness about being a Polish refugee and having a disfigured hand, she took up table tennis. She became such a skilled player that she competed in the 1953 and 1957 Maccabiah Games in Israel, an international Jewish athletic event similar to the Olympics. In 1957, she moved to Israel, and in 1968, she immigrated to the United States. She eventually married Richard Peabody, worked in administration at various companies, and raised a family. She has two sons and two granddaughters, whom she calls the light of her life.

Halina Peabody, who lives in Bethesda, Maryland, is one of more than 80 Holocaust survivors who volunteer at the United States Holocaust Memorial Museum, where she speaks about her experiences to school-children and to other groups. "All of us survivors wish for the same thing," she says. "We look forward to the day when people can practice their religion free from bigotry and hatred."

"I'm Not Ready to Die!"

===

Eddie Weinstein

"Attention! Attention!" announced the police, stalking through the Jewish ghetto in Losice, Poland. "Everyone, without exception, must leave home and report immediately to the market square for deportation. You have one hour to assemble. Anyone who disobeys this order will be shot."

Ever since Germany had invaded Poland in 1939 and made life unbearable for Jews, teenager Eddie Weinstein had seen firsthand that the heartless enemy didn't need any excuse to kill a Jew. The lanky, wavy-haired 15-year-old slave laborer had witnessed fellow workers clubbed, whipped, and shot for no reason.

Eddie and his brother, Israel, who was two years younger, rushed to the cramped one-room apartment that they and their parents, Asher and Leah, had been sharing with four other people for much of the previous nine months. During that time, German soldiers had expelled more than 8,000 Jews from their homes in the surrounding area and shoved them into the Losice ghetto, where food and the necessities of life were scarce and death was common.

Like everyone else, the boys and their mother quickly gathered up clothing and other items they thought essential for their deportation to an unknown place. Eddie's father was not there. The last they heard from him, he was toiling in a slave labor camp. There was no way of knowing if they would ever see or hear from him again.

By midmorning of August 22, 1942, the market square was swarming with thousands of frightened Jews, each carrying a stuffed suitcase or a bundle tied in a sheet or tablecloth. Eddie wondered, *Where are we going? Russia? A Polish work camp? Germany?*

Women, children, the ill, and the elderly were thrown into horse-drawn wagons with their belongings and left first. But because there wasn't enough room, many of them had to go on foot. The men and teenagers marched out of town in columns of hundreds of people 8 to 12 abreast. Wrapped in a cloud of dust so dense it was hard to see or breathe, the captives were forced to run while being spat upon, beaten, and kicked by machine gun–toting soldiers. Some people panicked and tried to flee only to get gunned down. Hundreds who didn't hustle fast enough were whipped or shot to death, speeding up and terrorizing the rest.

For hours in the blazing sun, Eddie and Israel stayed together. When the tired, parched Jews reached the town of

Mordy ten miles from Losice, bodies and empty suitcases were strewn along the streets.

"The Jews of Mordy have already been deported," Eddie said.

"Look," said Israel, pointing to non-Jewish Poles who were carting furniture and boxes out of houses. "They're looting the Jews' homes."

"The same thing no doubt is happening back in Losice."

As dust clogged their nostrils and throats, people begged for water, but the soldiers ignored them. Eventually, the captives caught up with the wagons. About 18 miles later, the soldiers halted the marchers but ordered the wagons and women to keep going. Leah was keeping pace behind a wagon filled with children when she passed Eddie. He tried to reach his mother, but an S.S. officer struck him in the head with a riding crop, barking, "Don't move or you die!"

"Eddie!" his mother shouted to her distraught son. "Stay with your brother!"

"Mother!" he cried out. Through his tears and the dust, he watched Leah shrink from sight. He wondered, *Will I ever see her again?*

The fast-paced march continued. After trudging another two miles, the Jews arrived at the ghetto in the town of Siedlce. Everywhere he looked in the evening light, Eddie saw bodies lying in the streets. The gruesome sights made him forget about his unquenchable thirst. The marchers were herded into a barbed-wire pen for the night—which turned into a night of terror as German troops callously shot into the crowd. Eddie and Israel huddled together, hearing the screams of the wounded and dying, who had been caught in the line of fire.

At dawn, Eddie saw dozens of bodies of Jews carried out and placed on carts. They had been killed during the night. He warned his brother not to do anything to attract attention because the guards were still shooting people who caught their eye—a man with a red beard, a girl in a colorful dress, a boy playing with a stick. And with every murder, the guards laughed.

The sun beat down on the parched captives, all craving a drink of water. But none was given. Late in the afternoon, they were marched to the railroad station. To ease their awful thirst, some scooped mud from puddles alongside the road and stuffed it in their mouths. A bullet put an end to their thirst and their lives. Others who broke ranks and sprinted toward nearby wells were cut down by gunfire.

Eventually, the soldiers allowed a fire truck to spray the people with water. Eddie and his brother opened their mouths wide, trying to catch every precious droplet in the mass shower. "Take off your shirt and get it wet," Eddie told his brother. "We'll squeeze out the water later, so we'll have something to drink."

In the huge mob, Eddie and Israel looked for their mother but couldn't find her, although someone told them she was still alive. Eddie bumped into his distraught aunt

Leah, who threw her arms around him and wept. "They killed your uncle Mottl," she wailed. "They shot him dead in the square in Siedlce."

Penned up with thousands of others for another night of terror, Eddie and Israel hoped and prayed that the occasional bullet fired into the crowd wouldn't strike them.

The following morning, a long freight train arrived. Hungry, thirsty, and weary, the Jews were shoved into 60 cattle cars. Eddie and Israel were among the first to get on. So many people were crammed inside their car that it was getting hard to breathe. Some passed out but couldn't fall to the floor because they were packed in so tightly.

"We're going to suffocate," gasped Eddie. "Israel, we've got to get out of here. Follow me." They climbed over people's heads and wriggled, rolled, and twisted their way to the front of the open door. "Let's try to get to another cattle car," Eddie told his brother. "The guards might shoot us, but it's better to get shot to death than die of suffocation."

The brothers jumped out of the overstuffed boxcar and into the swarm of people still waiting to be pushed into other cars. The boys hopped into one that was nearly filled to capacity and closed the door before it became insufferably crowded.

Soon the long train began to move. About four hours later, it stopped on a railway spur outside Treblinka II. No one knew what the place was. *A prison? A way station? The end of the line?* What they did know was that dehydration and heat exhaustion were killing dozens in each cattle car.

Desperately thirsty people broke open the window bars of the boxcars, jumped out, and staggered toward a water pump. They were all gunned down as the Weinstein brothers watched helplessly.

The locomotive towed the first 20 cars into the camp. The brothers' car remained stationary through the afternoon, so Eddie slumped in a corner and fell asleep. When it was dark, he awoke to hear people crying and praying.

"We're inside the camp," Israel told him in a trembling voice. "I think they're going to shoot us when they open the doors."

"Hear our prayers, O God," a young woman pleaded.

"God isn't here," wept an elderly man.

Many hugged their loved ones, convinced they would be murdered at any moment. In their despair, some people pounded their heads against the walls of the car. Eddie pushed his way toward a small peephole and looked out. He felt like throwing up. Bodies were piled all along the camp's train platform. He thought, *We're going to die now.*

When the doors were opened, the guards bellowed, "Get out! Get out, you scum! Move! Move!" They slammed their rifle butts into the Jews' backs. Some could barely walk. Others tumbled out. "Men and older boys to the right! Women, children, and the old to the left!"

The bleak camp was surrounded by a barbed-wire fence covered with tree branches to block any view from the outside. Tall watchtowers rose from each corner. Wooden barracks and warehouses formed a U in the center of the reception area.

Eddie and Israel moved to the right and watched those in the left column disappear through a large gate. *Why are so few people coming out of the cars?* he wondered. *They were packed.* Eddie got his answer minutes later when he and the other young men were ordered to remove the dead from the cattle cars. In every car he found bodies.

He was beyond shock, beyond despair. It was too hard for his brain to process. Here was the body of the baker and over there, that of a neighbor. *Oh, God, no. Not Esther. And her whole family!* Eddie's cousin Esther Yocheved, her three young daughters, and her husband were curled up together, dead. Lying nearby he spotted the bodies of Uncle Matis and his wife and daughter.

Working in pairs, the young men were part of a group of slave workers who carried corpses out of the cattle cars and piled them on the platform. The bodies were then taken to a pit dug by other workers for a mass grave. Hour after hour, the captives brought out the dead. There was no time to think. No time to mourn. "Work, work, or I'll shoot!" hissed the guards.

Eddie, Israel, and the others toiled all night under the searchlights. Many collapsed and died from exhaustion and were dragged off just as they had done earlier with other bodies. Worn out and dehydrated, the brothers stole a few minutes of rest by hiding under a nearby pile of rags until guards discovered them and threatened to kill them if they didn't get back to work.

Word spread that they were all going to die soon—today, tomorrow, maybe next week—because Treblinka was an extermination camp.

At sunrise, a bulldozer began to excavate three large deep pits because there were so many bodies. Later the brothers and their fellow workers were each given a small cup of lukewarm water, not nearly enough to slake their thirst. Then they were taken back to the railroad spur to load onto a flatcar the bodies of the Jews who had been shot the day before when they sought water to drink. The laborers worked on the run without a moment's rest. Those who didn't move fast enough were struck with rifle butts.

Two guards ordered Eddie and three young men to walk across a nearby shallow stream. Seeing the water, the four sank to their knees and eagerly swigged until the guards stuck rifles in their faces.

On the other side of the stream, Eddie spotted the bodies of two men who had been shot during an escape attempt. One of them, whom Eddie recognized as a well-off merchant, was still clutching a handful of banknotes. *He was probably trying to buy off his murderer,* Eddie thought. The workers lugged the two corpses to the flatcar.

After all the bodies were loaded, the workers were taken back to the camp. While unloading the corpses, Eddie learned from other inmates that most of the new prisoners had already been gassed—especially the elderly, children, and women. Among the dead, the brothers were convinced, was their mother, Leah.

Around noon, an S.S. officer arrived with two prisoners, each carrying a pail of water. As the workers lined up for a sip, Eddie saw the S.S. man reach for his handgun and pull the trigger. The bullet ripped into the right side of Eddie's chest four inches from his armpit and exited out his back. As he crumpled to the ground, he didn't feel any pain at first.

Israel cried out in alarm and rushed to him. A prisoner leaned over Eddie, who was now moaning because the pain grew sharper. "He's still moving," said the inmate. "Maybe we should ask the S.S. man to finish him off. Why should this boy suffer?"

Wincing, Eddie whispered, "Yes, do that." *This terrible camp is no place for the healthy, let alone for the wounded,* he told himself. *Either way, my time is up.*

"No! No!" cried Israel. When the guards weren't looking, he dragged Eddie about 100 yards into a wooden building where slave laborers were sorting clothing that had belonged to the dead and opening packages that the victims had brought. He placed Eddie on a pile of clothes and began to sob.

"Stop crying," Eddie muttered. "It's my time to die."

"No, it isn't!" Appealing to the workers, Israel said, "Find a towel so I can clean the wound."

A worker rummaged through the clothing and returned with a large shirt and a towel. Israel removed Eddie's bloodstained shirt, wrapped the wound in a towel, and dressed Eddie in the stolen shirt.

The pain was getting worse. "I can't stand this anymore," Eddie groaned. "Find an S.S. man and tell him to put an end to my agony."

Israel began to cry again. "Please don't talk that way. We've just lost Mother, and we don't know if Father is still alive. Now you, too, want to abandon me. It's more than I can bear. If you die, then I no longer wish to live."

"You have to survive," Eddie urged. "You'll be the only member of our family who could avenge our deaths when the Germans lose the war. My luck has run out. But you still have a chance. You're young and healthy. You have to carry on."

"I'll try," said Israel, wiping away his tears. "But please, Eddie, don't die."

After carefully covering Eddie under a pile of rags to hide him from the guards, Israel brought him water. Then Israel joined the workers who were opening packages. Someone found a bottle of iodine and gave it to Israel, who poured it into Eddie's wound to prevent infection. Eddie clenched his teeth and whimpered. "I can't stand the pain."

When he heard that a doctor was hiding in the next building, Israel and a cousin dragged Eddie there, but the doctor had left. The long wooden structure was stuffed to the rafters with parcels and bundles bearing the names and addresses of people from the Polish town of Radom. Concealed among the clothes was Eddie's friend Julke Goldberg, who had been shot in the elbow. Julke's brother Sane was hiding in a nearby pile with a few other Jews. Israel put Eddie next to Julke and covered Eddie's body with clothes and several bundles. "I'll go look for water for you," Israel said. "I'll be right back."

Minutes later, a guard barged into the building and shouted, "Whoever is hiding in here, get out now or I'll shoot!"

I can't obey the order even if I wanted to, Eddie told himself. *Lie still and don't breathe.* The guard stomped through the pile of clothes and bundles, looking for hidden prisoners. Every time he found one, he shot the prisoner dead at point-blank range. Eddie could hear the guard coming his way. Closer and closer. *He's going to step right on me!*

The guard's foot came down inches from Eddie's head. "I see you, you Jewish piece of filth!"

At least he'll put me out of my misery. Eddie waited for death to come. The guard fired his gun and moved on. *I'm not shot! He killed someone else!* By now, the pain and stress were so severe that Eddie passed out.

When he regained consciousness later that afternoon, he heard machine-gun fire and screams outside the building. Julke crawled toward Eddie and whispered, "You're still alive. I wish that were true for Sane. He went out to look for water, and a guard followed him and killed him and some others who were hiding here."

"My brother? What about Israel?" Eddie asked.

"I don't know. He hasn't returned." Julke squeezed Eddie's hand and said, "I had a dream that you and I survived."

"I hope it comes true." Julke's dream strengthened Eddie's resolve to survive.

Over the next two days, Eddie lay in terrible pain, yearning for water, food, and his brother. All he consumed were a few sugar cubes and mouthfuls of vinegar that a worker had found. Julke hadn't left the building, either, and was getting weaker.

After three days without water, Eddie peered through a crack in a wall and saw that workers were being given some. He thought, *I can't stand it any longer. I have to take a chance. I'll die without water.*

Praying that he wouldn't be noticed, Eddie stepped out of the building. He could barely move his right arm or tolerate the excruciating pain. Trying to act normal, he mingled with workers who were clearing the area of corpses. Each time the workers brought a body to a pit, they received a little water. Eddie tried to join the corpse draggers so he could get a drink, but they turned him away. He didn't look like someone who could help. He looked more like one of the dead who were being tossed into the pits.

Eventually, he teamed up with three others and together they carried away bodies in return for a sip of water. Occasionally, soldiers fired in the air to speed up the work. Eddie took advantage of the commotion one time to sneak back into the building and bring water to Julke.

The next day—a week since Eddie and his fellow Jews had been forced out of Losice—workers started boarding up the entrances to the building where he was hiding. "We have to leave," he whispered to Julke. "If we stay here, we'll die of thirst or hunger."

"I'm staying," Julke declared. "I'm afraid to leave because the bandage on my elbow is visible, and if the guards see I'm wounded, they'll kill me. You go. Good luck."

Posing as a worker, Eddie slipped out of the building and went searching for his brother. He spotted Gedalia Rosenzweig, a school friend, and asked him, "Have you seen Israel? Is he still alive?"

Gedalia put his hand on Eddie's shoulder and shook his head. "I'm sorry, Eddie," Gedalia replied. "There are so few of us left. The Germans selected fifty prisoners, including seven of us boys from the Losice transport for clothes-sorting duty. All the others were murdered. Israel was one of them."

Eddie closed his eyes in grief.

"Eddie, come work with us. It's your only hope of surviving."

As a way for the guards to identify them, all the clothes sorters had been given a triangle-shaped piece of red cloth that they sewed to their right trouser leg. Gedalia found a red shirt and tore a portion into a triangle and attached it to Eddie's pants with a safety pin. "The Germans will never know there's one extra clothes sorter," Gedalia said.

116

But at the end of the day, an S.S. officer counted the workers and found too many, so he ordered them to line up. Holding a list, he began a roll call, checking off each name. When he stood in front of Eddie and asked his name, the teenager froze. *What am I going to do?* he thought. *If I give him my real name, I'm dead.* In a panic, Eddie answered "Gedalia Rosenzweig." The soldier checked off the name and moved on. *What have I done? What happens when he gets to Gedalia?*

In an incredible stroke of luck, the officer was called away before he reached the real Gedalia and never came back. The workers were sent to their barracks, and Eddie sighed with relief. *I'm still alive. But for how long?* The prisoners lived not only from day to day but from minute to minute. The horror only grew worse.

From others, Eddie learned what he had suspected since his arrival: Treblinka was a death camp designed to kill thousands a day. When the deportees arrived at the rate of 20 cattle cars at a time, an S.S. officer lied to them, claiming Treblinka was a stopover and that they would be sent to various labor camps. But first they had to take a shower and have their clothes disinfected. Any money and valuables in their possessions were to be handed over for safekeeping and returned to them after they had showered. The women and children were sent to their undressing building while the men took off their clothes in another area.

The naked Jews were then ushered through a 100-yard-long "tube," a six-foot-high camouflaged pathway made up of earthen mounds and barbed wire. (The Germans called it the road to heaven.) At the end of the tube was a long brick building that contained what the people believed were the "showers" but were really the gas chambers.

Once the victims were locked inside, deadly carbon monoxide gas was pumped in, killing everyone within 20 to 30 minutes. Their bodies were removed from the chambers and taken to burial or cremation pits. Between 2,000 and 3,000 Jews—those who arrived in 20 cattle cars—could be exterminated within four hours.

The Germans kept alive about 700 Jews to work in the camp. The empty cattle cars were towed out of the station, and a short time later a locomotive arrived with another 20 cars. The process was repeated until the entire transport was emptied.

To hide any signs of bloodshed and death, the workers cleaned the railway platform, covering it with burned-out coal and laying fresh branches along the fence. But the stench of charred corpses hung in the air.

Despite the agonizing pain in his right side and useless right arm, Eddie joined the workers in a large field within sight of the gas chambers and the burning pits. With his left hand, Eddie laid coats, dresses, and underwear on a sheet that had been spread out. When it was full, Gedalia tied the corners into a bundle and took it over to a stack.

In the barracks at night, workers tried to bolster one another's morale. Eddie desperately wanted to believe that the world knew about the mass murdering of Jews and would put an end to this horrifying genocide. Other prisoners, convinced the world didn't know or didn't care, gave up hope. They hanged themselves with their belts at night. Eddie helped haul their bodies away in the morning.

He learned that the building where he had hid the first few days had been cleaned out of all concealed Jews, who were then executed. *Poor Julke*, Eddie thought. *He should have left with me. Now I can only hope that half his dream will come true.*

One day, five S.S. officers showed up, accompanied by Treblinka's second-in-command, Kurt Hubert Franz, a former waiter. The prisoners had nicknamed him *Lalka*, Polish for "doll," because he was handsome, clean-shaven, perfectly dressed, and wore spit-shined boots. He gave the visiting S.S. men a tour of the death factory, proudly showing off its ghastly features.

Several minutes later, as Eddie and the workers sorted clothes, two guards ordered Eddie and about three dozen others to stand up and form a column. Eddie had been in Treblinka long enough to know what that meant. *They're going to kill us!* As the selected workers rose, Eddie sneakily backed off and, without being detected, rejoined those who had not been picked. The column was then led toward one of the pits. All were shot and killed there.

Eddie and the surviving workers had seen so much cruelty and death that they didn't say a word. They grimly went on with their tasks in silence. Eddie wondered, *How could those Germans carry out such atrocities and return home at the end of the day and kiss their children, eat dinner, and sleep soundly?* Even though the weather was stiflingly hot, the inhumanity he witnessed made him shudder. *Somehow, some way, I have to escape.*

Eddie and Gedalia became one of 20 pairs of workers who cleaned out railroad cars after the passengers had been removed. Someone came up with a clever idea that spared some lives, if only for a few extra days. When each train stopped, several workers handed their brooms to some of the new arrivals, who then posed as workers. The original workers, who were identified by the red patches on their clothing, removed the trash while the newcomers swept out the cars. Afterward, the newcomers mixed with the real workers and returned the brooms. At *Appell,* the numbers didn't match up with the guards' list of workers' names. Sometimes the guards ignored the difference. Other times they took out their anger and frustration by shooting workers from both groups.

"The Germans don't care about our ruse one way or the other," Gedalia told Eddie. "It doesn't matter to them who drags out the bodies and who sorts the clothing. We're all going to die in the end."

"Well, I don't intend to die," Eddie declared. "Not here."

Workers seldom lasted long. Many were sent to the gas chambers every day, often picked at random or because they were too weak to carry out their jobs. Replacements were selected from the newcomers. Eddie had been able to dodge death for nearly two weeks and was surprised that he was still alive.

But then guards selected several dozen workers, including Eddie, and ordered them to undress. *They're sending us to the gas chamber,* he told himself. *I'm not ready to die. There's got to be a way out of this. Think! Think!* His eyes darted left and right and then locked onto workers who were digging a new trench to serve as a latrine behind the barracks. *That's my only hope.*

He strode over to the workers, but an armed guard blocked his path, snarling, "Where do you think you're going?"

Without hesitation, Eddie answered, "I've been sent to work here."

The guard pointed his rifle at Eddie's chest and snapped, "You're lying."

Keep bluffing. Don't back down. "My orders are to help dig the latrine."

Jakob Müller, a friend from Losice who was one of the workers, quickly figured out what was happening and shouted, "Eddie, get over here and back to work!" Grumbling, the guard let Eddie pass.

When he reached the workers, Eddie whispered to Jakob, "Thanks. You saved my life—at least for today."

The next morning, the guards chose dozens of workers at random and led them toward the gas chambers. Jakob Müller was one of them.

That afternoon, an empty freight train arrived. Eddie and several other workers were ordered for the first time to load bundles of victims' belongings into the cattle cars. Eddie was elated. "This is our chance to escape!" he told Gedalia and Michael Fischmann, a 24-year-old from Losice. "We'll sneak into a car and hide under the suitcases and bundles."

"What about money?" asked Gedalia.

"I've collected gold coins from the victims' belongings," Michael replied. "I've hid the coins in money belts and buried them in the sand near the train platform." A short while later, out of view, he dug up the belts and handed one to Eddie and another to Gedalia.

Several times that day, Eddie tried to enter a cattle car, but the loaders wouldn't let him in. "Are you crazy?" one of the workers told him. "Before the guards lock each car, they check to make sure no one is hiding inside. If they catch a stowaway, they'll kill him and everyone who loaded that car. Now go away!"

But Eddie refused to give up. When the second group of cattle cars was brought into the camp, he found two husky teenagers from Losice who were loading it. He knew one of them, Leizer Mordski. Eddie revealed the escape plan to Leizer, who agreed to look the other way.

As dozens of workers hauled bundles, Eddie put one on his shoulder and headed for the cattle car. *This has to work. . . . It just has to.* For him, it was escape or die. The suspense was so great that he forgot the pain in his right arm. When the car was filled halfway, he carried a bundle inside. But instead of going back out, he hid under the clothes in a corner near a window. Soon Michael and Gedalia took cover with him.

The three lay still, anxious and tense, sweating from the heat and lack of air, but mainly from fear of being discovered. In the meantime, the workers added more bundles to the car until there was no room left. When they finished, Leizer called a guard to inspect the car. The trio remained still as the soldier climbed in and rummaged through the clothes. Eddie closed his eyes, hoping his wildly pounding heart wouldn't give him away. "Everything's fine," the guard announced, jumping onto the platform.

After the heavy door slammed shut and was locked, Eddie and his two comrades stayed hidden under the bundles in total darkness for about half an hour before the locomotive lurched and the cars began to move forward. Only then did the three feel it was safe to crawl out from their hiding places.

Eddie peered through the window. As the train platform faded, so, too, did the tension that had gripped his body. "We're on the outside," he announced to the others. "We've escaped from Treblinka! We've escaped!" He could think of nothing else—not where they were headed or how they would get out of the locked car before the Germans opened it—only, *We've escaped!*

The three had sneaked out of the factory of death on September 10 after surviving 17 days of torment.

To their dismay, the train stopped for the night just a mile from the camp. The young men buried themselves under the bundles and remained quiet, although Eddie kept coughing. Around midnight, several men talking in Polish opened the door. Terrified, Eddie thought, *They must have heard me coughing and now they're searching for us.* The doors of other cars were opened, too. After a nerve-racking hour, Eddie heard the Poles leave.

Early the next morning when the train began to move again, the escapees emerged from under the mounds of clothes. Seeing that some of the bundles had been removed, Michael said, "Now I know what happened last night after the train stopped. The Poles opened the cattle cars and stole clothes to sell on the black market."

At the next train stop, Eddie peeked through a crack and saw a sign for a town that he knew was south of Treblinka. "Good news!" he whispered. "We're traveling toward home!"

Once again, the three hid under the bundles as the car door opened and someone else swiped more clothes. Unfortunately, the person then locked the door. A few miles later, the train slowed to a crawl and several men hustled alongside it, opening the doors and snatching bundles. After the thieves had taken clothes from the escapees' car and moved on to the next one, Michael said, "Let's jump now!"

They squeezed through a small window on the opposite side of the car, dropped to the ground, and fled into the forest. Soon they came upon an old man who was grazing his cows. Realizing they were Jews, he warned them not to enter the next town because S.S. troops were moving into the area.

"Let's go to the work camp in Siedlce," Gedalia suggested. "Two of my brothers are working there. It's safer working for the Germans than being on the run."

"My father was working there when I was deported," Eddie said. "Maybe, just maybe, he's still alive."

They detoured around villages and stayed off roads, hiking instead along narrow paths in the woods and fields until they came to the town of Mokobody, where workers from the camp were smashing boulders to use in making a road. Without being seen by guards, the three escapees joined the workers shortly before all were taken to the camp on tractor-pulled wagons.

To his unbridled joy, Eddie learned that his father, Asher, was alive, toiling as a gardener for the German camp staff. When the boy entered the barrack, Asher stared at him in disbelief and then collapsed in his arms, sobbing uncontrollably. Eddie wanted to cry, too, having found his father at last. But no tears of happiness would come.

Instead, his eyes watered with grief. "Mother and Israel are dead and so are all our relatives from Losice," he blurted out. "They were murdered at Treblinka." Eddie then revealed in gruesome detail the horrors he had witnessed at the death camp. Father and son talked through the night, and by morning they felt blessed that they were still alive and together again.

Eventually, they escaped from the camp and looked for

someone who would hide them. For a fee, the manager of a fishpond let them build a bunker on the property and provided them with soup and bread. During the next year and a half, Eddie and his father remained concealed in their hideaway, going out at night to bathe and forage for food.

Late one July night in 1944, they crawled out of the bunker to the deafening sounds of trucks, tanks, and shouts. The German army, which had been retreating in Poland from the advancing Russians, was mounting a last stand. "The Germans are establishing a defensive line too close to our hideout," Asher said. "They'll soon find it. We need to get out of here."

Eddie and his father spent the night hiding among the stacks of grain drying in a large field. The next morning, German soldiers spotted them. Fleeing for their lives, Eddie and Asher sprinted in opposite directions. Eddie dashed into a potato field and lay motionless on his stomach in a furrow where he heard shouts and shooting throughout the day. He didn't move until about 11 P.M. when all had been silent for several hours. Then he retraced his steps. In the moonlight, he saw that virtually all the stacks in the grain field had been trampled. *They surely found Father and killed him,* he thought. *I just want to find his body so I can give him a proper burial.*

Making his way toward the middle of the field, he heard someone whisper from inside one of the few remaining stacks, "Eddie, Eddie, is that you?"

The boy's heart leaped in elation. "Father?"

They fell into each other's arms and wept.

"I was sure you were dead," said Eddie.

"And I thought the same about you. When we fled, I hid in the sheaves. The Germans scattered almost all of them but skipped the one I was in. I hadn't moved since then."

They walked through the night before lying down in a thick field of rye that had not yet been reaped. "The Russians will liberate Poland any day now," Asher predicted. "And then we'll be free." Suddenly, shooting erupted all around them. They were caught in another gun battle so they lay flat, hoping the fighting would end soon. It did, but then they heard approaching footsteps. *Please be the Russians, please be the Russians,* Eddie prayed.

"Get up! Get up!"

Eddie's heart sank. The gruff voice was speaking German. Shaking in fear, the boy and his father stood up and were immediately surrounded by 15 soldiers, all aiming their rifles at them.

They're going to kill us, Eddie thought. *We were so close to freedom. After all Father and I have been through, to die like this.*

"What were you doing in this field?" the sergeant demanded.

"We were looking for farmwork during the harvest season. When the gunfire started, we ran here to keep from being hit," Eddie replied.

"Why would you choose to run into a grain field?" the sergeant asked.

Without giving any real thought to his answer, Eddie explained, "It's so thick that I thought it would slow the bullets before they reached us."

The soldiers looked at one another and burst into laughter. Hooting and slapping his knee, the sergeant turned to his soldiers and said, "What an idiot he is! So naïve. He thinks rye can stop bullets."

Eddie tried to smile, but all he could think about was, *What are they going to do to us?*

Eddie and Asher floated with relief when they were released and told to walk toward town. Unfortunately, the shooting soon became intense again, so they hid along a creek bed. When the fighting stopped, they looked up and saw five soldiers clutching machine guns. "No, not again!" Eddie cried. But then he noticed they were wearing uniforms he had never seen before.

His father gazed in wide-eyed amazement and said in Russian, "You are Russians, right?"

The leader of the group nodded. "Yes, we now occupy this area."

Asher raced over to him and hugged him, gushing, "Oh, thank you! Thank you!"

The soldiers led Eddie and Asher to a nearby farm, where another Russian officer welcomed them. "Who are you?" he asked.

"I am Asher Weinstein. And this is my son, Eddie. We are Jews who have been hiding from the Germans."

"Well, you don't have to hide anymore," the Russian said. "You're free."

As tears trickled down his cheeks, Asher asked, "What is today's date?"

"It's July 31, 1944," the officer replied.

Asher threw his arm around his son and said, "Remember this date, Eddie. It is the day you and I were reborn."

═══

One month later, Eddie joined the Polish army and fought against the Germans until the war ended the next year. After suffering Germany's brutal and bloody persecution, he was proud to do his part to defeat the Nazis.

Of the estimated 40,000 Jews originally living in Siedlce, only 200 survived the Holocaust. Eddie's friends Gedalia Rosenweig and Michael Fischmann, who had escaped from Treblinka with him, had gone into hiding to wait out the war but were discovered and killed.

Leizer Mordski, who helped the trio escape from Treblinka, later sneaked out of the death camp the same way they did. He hid for a year and a half in the forest but then was captured and killed only three weeks before the area was liberated.

Jakob Müller, whom Eddie last saw being led toward the gas chambers, wasn't murdered after all. He was put on another work detail and managed to survive in Treblinka for almost a year. On August 2, 1943, he took part in an uprising when prisoners seized weapons from the camp armory and stormed the main gate. Many were killed by machine-gun fire. More than 300 escaped, including Jakob, but 200 of them were eventually tracked down and killed. Jakob hid in the forest until liberation and then immigrated to Uruguay.

Before Treblinka II was destroyed, an estimated 900,000 Jews were murdered there. Fewer than 100 are known to have successfully escaped.

Eddie and his father ended up in a European displaced-persons camp, where they each found a wife. In 1949, they immigrated to the United States and settled in Brooklyn, New York. Eddie operated a sewing machine for a company that made raincoats. Ten years later, after saving enough money, he started his own business, Eddie's Knitting Mills, which he ran successfully for 45 years. Eddie, whose first wife, Jean, died in 1984, lives with his second wife, Judith, in Little Neck, New York. He has two sons, both Ph.D.s, and seven grandchildren.

Eddie, who often speaks about the Holocaust to school groups, has written a book about his experiences called 17 Days in Treblinka.

"Run! Run for Your Lives!"

===

Gideon Frieder

At age seven, Gideon Frieder was too young at first to realize that he and his family were in mortal danger. But he knew not to walk on certain streets, because other children would throw rocks at him and call him vile names. Being ridiculed and persecuted was a way of life for Jews living in Slovakia—a landlocked country in central Europe run by a pro-Nazi government during World War II.

Like other nations dominated by Germany during the war, Slovakia established inhumane laws and began shipping Jews to concentration camps and death camps. Gideon's father, Abraham, one of the country's most influential rabbis, saved thousands of Jews by negotiating directly with the government. He helped stem the mass deportations and organized relief efforts for those held prisoner. But as the Nazis gained a stranglehold on the country, he no longer was able to protect his fellow Jews. In fact, he became a marked man.

In summer 1944, an alliance of 60,000 Slovak soldiers, 20,000 partisans, and thousands of Jews, Russians, and other anti-Nazis planned a massive uprising. For his own safety and that of his family, Abraham went underground to continue his efforts of saving Jews. If he was caught, he and his family would be imprisoned and likely killed. Gideon's grandparents had already been deported and murdered.

Over the next several weeks, Gideon saw his father only during brief visits when Abraham sneaked home. One day a strange man entered the house and surprised the boy by hugging and kissing his mother. Not until the man spoke did Gideon realize it was his father. The boy had always seen him with a big, flowing beard. But Abraham had shaved his thick facial hair so he wouldn't be recognized by the enemy. Although it was a joyous occasion, Abraham brought grim news: Tens of thousands of well-armed German soldiers were marching from the south of Slovakia to crush the freedom fighters' uprising. Gideon, his mother, Ruzena, and his four-year-old sister, Gita, would have to leave their home in Nové Mesto immediately.

"You are going on a ride with your mother," Abraham told the children. "It's all arranged. I won't be going with you because I am needed elsewhere. But I will see you later. Everything will be all right."

They packed up a few clothes and other supplies and then hid in the back of an ambulance. Rather than head north, where many Jews and freedom fighters were fleeing, the ambulance went south toward the German lines so it wouldn't draw suspicion from the enemy. Then it turned east and eventually north.

When the Frieders arrived at their destination, they were warned that the Germans were searching for—and killing—Jews. Gideon and his mother and sister fled into the forest, where a local ranger gave them food and milk. After spending the night in a cabin, they paid a farmer to take them by wagon to an area defended by the partisans. But because the partisans were engaged in a pitched battle with the Germans, the family was forced to turn back. The next day, they reached the town of Bánovce, where the partisans fed them. When a large German force headed their way, the Frieders escaped with the partisans. Gideon, Gita, and Ruzena were placed in a broken-down car that was pulled by another car. The rope broke twice along the way, and they barely managed to reach safety—but only momentarily. Wherever they went, they had to evacuate because the undermanned and poorly equipped fighters weren't strong or experienced enough to stop the powerful enemy's advance.

The family eventually reached the city of Banská Bystrica, the nerve center of the uprising. Refugees and fleeing Jews poured into the area, filling up all available hotels and rooming houses. Gideon overheard reports that special German forces and the Hlinka Guard—Slovakia's pro-Nazi militia—were slaughtering Jews, peasants, and workers and burning their villages and towns. All Jews, whether they were innocent or not, were accused of being rebels and murdered on the spot.

By October 1944, the uprising was faltering badly. Banská Bystrica was put on full military alert after German and Hlinka Guard forces closed in for a final assault on the city. When the freedom fighters made plans to flee to the mountains, Jews who came to the city for protection were filled with despair. They had nowhere to go.

With Gideon and Gita by her side, Ruzena went to Jewish partisan Henry Herzog and begged, "Please, take my children and me along."

"The mountains are no place for a woman and small children," he replied. "It will be snowing and freezing in those mountains. You and your children aren't prepared for that. We face dangerous, hard conditions."

"We stand no chance of remaining alive if we stay here," she insisted. "Where will we hide? How will we survive? You can't leave us behind."

Herzog looked into the children's innocent faces and the pleading eyes of their desperate mother. "Okay," he said. "Be ready to leave first thing in the morning. Be prepared for bad weather and don't take unnecessary heavy loads. Only food and warm clothing."

Before daybreak on October 27, the Frieders joined hundreds of Jewish and non-Jewish partisans, refugees, and soldiers—some riding in cars, horse-drawn buggies, and military trucks hauling heavy armament. There were few women and children. The civilians—including Ruzena, who carried Gita, and Gideon—walked in a long, slow line in a cold, light rain. Wearing the typical garb of young boys in the region, Gideon was dressed in a wool sweater, shorts with suspenders, and thick wool socks.

With grenades strapped to their belts and ammunition draped across their chests, the freedom fighters carried their guns upside down to keep the barrels from filling with water. Because the uprising was all but over, the grim-faced group was in no mood to cheer up any of the children in the frigid, wet darkness.

Everyone was on the road toward the Staré Hory Valley because it was the only way out. Behind them, the Germans were pushing toward Banská Bystrica. The road, barely wide enough for two small cars, was bordered by a stream on one side and a sloping meadow on the other.

When it grew light, much of the lengthy column had reached the narrow valley. To his left and right, Gideon saw the mountains rising, but he couldn't see their tops because of the low, drizzling clouds. Like everyone else, Gideon was wet and shivering, but no one complained. Their only thought was to get as far away as possible from Banská Bystrica, because the Germans would soon find out about this mass exodus and try to attack it.

Gideon didn't fully grasp the gravity of the situation. In a way, it seemed like an adventure because the family had been going from one place to another, and he had met lots of interesting people. Besides, he didn't always have time to brush his teeth or wash behind his ears, which, in his childish mind, was a good thing.

When the column bogged down, he took advantage of the holdup by walking down to the stream. He began tossing stones into the water but stopped when he heard a strange, frightening sound — high-pitched screeching from above. He looked up and saw several German dive bombers known as *Stuka Junkers* swooping down into the valley. The planes "shrieked" because each Stuka was fitted with a small siren on the undercarriage to add a terrifying and demoralizing sound to the whine of its engine and the whistle of its falling bombs.

Deafening explosions shook the ground at the entrance and exit to the valley. Then machine-gun fire from the planes strafed the road.

"Run!" people yelled. "Run for your lives!"

Panic-stricken men, women, and children raced in all directions. But there was no escape. They were trapped like a school of fish in a net because the bombing had blocked both ends of the valley. The people and the vehicles were completely exposed and hemmed in on the open road.

Gideon stood motionless, seeing more bombs bursting and more machine guns blasting, and hearing the screams of those hit from shrapnel and bullets.

"Find cover!" a partisan shouted. "Get away from the road!"

Gideon snapped out of his momentary paralysis and dashed after his mother, who was still clutching Gita. When he caught up with them, Ruzena shouted, "Run toward the trees!" They rushed up a small rising meadow where several trees held at least some hope of cover. Just as they neared the other side of the meadow, Gideon heard a plane's machine gun firing from behind.

His right leg crumpled under him, and he tumbled to the ground. As he dropped, his mother collapsed and his sister fell out of her grasp. Burying his face in the wet grass, the boy remained still until the bombing and strafing ended. He didn't move for another few minutes, fearing that the planes would turn around and come back to continue their deadly spree. While he waited, he heard the moans and cries of the wounded.

When he figured it was safe to get up, Gideon crawled near the base of a large tree where his mother was lying on her back with her eyes open.

"Mama, are you all right?" he asked. When she failed to respond, he began to shake her. "Mama, please say something!" He became more frightened as he shook her again, harder this time. "Why won't you move?"

Then he hobbled to Gita, who was sprawled on her stomach. He leaned over his sister and gently pushed her. "Gita? Wake up, Gita. Please, wake up!" He turned her over. Her eyes were closed and she wasn't breathing.

In shock, he returned to his mother and pleaded with her to talk to him. Tears pooled in his eyes. "Get up, Mama. Get up."

Suddenly, he felt a pair of strong hands lift him from under his arms. "Come with me, Gideon." It was Herzog.

"No, I want to stay here with my mama and my sister."

"We will come for them later. You need to go with me now for your own safety." Herzog picked him up and carried him to the tree line.

From there, Gideon gazed in horror at the bloody scene in the valley. Dozens upon dozens of bodies lay at odd angles like rag dolls that had been tossed to the ground. The injured cried out for help. Survivors walked around in dazed grief or tried to comfort the wounded. The road was clogged with burning vehicles, dead horses, overturned wagons, and bundles that the trapped people had shed while fleeing for cover.

The screams of pain and the sight of so many dead and wounded terrified Gideon. All he could see was carnage. Behind him and ahead of him, countless family tragedies unfolded. He looked around and searched for some familiar faces among those wounded. He had no heart to look at the dead. Survivors were giving help wherever they could, but there were too few medical supplies and too many wounded. Whenever they found a dead comrade or civilian, they covered the victim's head and moved away.

Gideon didn't see that the partisans had carried the bodies of his mother and sister to the side and covered them up.

"The Germans might come back," Herzog told his men. "We can't escape by continuing our march through the valley."

The survivors decided to abandon the road that had brought so much death and pain. They chose to follow a steep path up one of the mountains. In single file, the devastated group slowly began the difficult hike up the mountain.

Gideon didn't think about all those who had died and weren't buried. He didn't look into the fearful eyes of the severely wounded who were left behind because there was nothing anyone could do for them. All Gideon cared about was being reunited with his mother and sister.

"Where's my mama?" Gideon cried out. "Where's Gita? Why don't I see them anywhere?"

No one had the heart to tell him the truth. But he knew in his gut they were dead. He just didn't want to believe it yet.

As the group trudged up the daunting slope, Gideon grew tired and fell asleep in the arms of one of the partisans. "What a tragedy for this boy," Herzog whispered to his comrades. "He's lost a mother and a sister, and he's separated from his father, who might not even be alive. And if his father is alive, the boy doesn't know where he is. It's up to us to look after him."

The higher they climbed, the colder it got. Rain turned to snow. When darkness arrived, the group set up camp and built a fire inside a ring of large stones. While the partisans took turns sitting around the blaze, Gideon joined the wounded, who were allowed to rest or sleep as long as they wanted.

When Gideon woke up during the night, he saw many campfires above and below him on the mountain. He overheard Herzog tell his comrades, "I only hope those people have their guards posted. All those fires can be seen by our enemies. They aren't too far behind us—and they know where we're going."

A Slovak air force officer who had joined the partisans told Herzog, "The German planes that attacked us were light bombers. After they ran out of bombs, I saw pilots throwing grenades at us. They tried to finish us off with their machine guns. It's a miracle that so many of us survived because we had no warning. Those planes appeared from nowhere. They were flying so low that our machine guns could have brought them down, but we didn't have time to set up our weapons."

Early the next morning, the group broke camp and began trekking farther up the mountain. A thick, wet snow was falling, causing slippery conditions. As Gideon hiked, his only thought was seeing his mother and sister again. Even though he knew Herzog wouldn't give it to him, he sought confirmation of their deaths from him.

"Where is my mother?" Gideon asked Herzog. "Why isn't she here with me? Where is my sister?"

Herzog sighed but couldn't bring himself to tell the whole truth. "Your mother and sister are in the valley," he said.

When the group stopped to rest, Herzog warned everyone, "Don't sit or stand in one place. If you must rest, do it only for short moments. Stamp your feet and move your arms around your body all the time. Otherwise you'll freeze to death."

As they trekked higher, Gideon passed several refugees who had rested too long. They were propped up against rocks and trees looking like they were asleep. But their sleep was eternal.

The boy noticed that many refugees ahead of him were dumping their heavier loads because it was so difficult to climb. The partisans went through the discarded bundles, and when they found guns and food, they gave them to the civilians marching with the group. Every gun and every bullet might be needed later.

Gideon heard explosions and machine-gun fire coming from far away—signs that the Germans were catching up to those who were the last to flee from Banská Bystrica, which was now in enemy hands.

Later that day, the partisans started building a bunker near the forest and posted guards. "The Germans aren't that far behind us," Herzog told his comrades. "They have experienced and well-trained mountain infantry—the best hunters and killers in the country."

Looking at Gideon, Herzog told his men, "This mountain is no place for a child. He needs a home." They decided to take the boy to the nearest safe hamlet, which meant going back down the mountain and across the valley of death.

A few days later, Herzog and three partisans escorted Gideon to the valley and the scene of the attack. The road looked different. The burned-out trucks had been pushed to the sides of the road, and the area was dotted with freshly dug shallow graves. There were no crosses, Stars of David, or helmets to mark the victims' final resting places.

The four hiked all day with Gideon until nightfall, when they spotted lights from the few homes in the remote hamlet of Bully, which was nestled at the foot of a mountain. The partisans watched the tiny village for a long time to make sure there weren't any enemy soldiers. Eventually, Gideon and the men walked down to the first house. Herzog knocked on the door as the others stood guard, shielding Gideon.

Displaying his grenades and weapon, Herzog entered the house and gave the two men and one woman who lived there a menacing glare. He wanted to scare the peasants so they would do exactly as he said. "What are your names?" he demanded.

The man of the house stepped forward and said, "I am Jozef Strycharczyk, and this is my wife, Paulina, and her brother, Jan Bula."

"We have a small boy with us," Herzog said gruffly. "He is alone because he lost his mother and sister in the Staré Hory massacre. His father is an important Jewish leader. This boy cannot continue living in the mountains with us and be exposed to this cold winter. He needs regular food and the warmth of a normal house. Somewhere not far from here his mother and his sister are buried in an unmarked grave. Somewhere in Slovakia is his father, who doesn't know about this tragedy. Ever since the Gestapo entered Slovakia, all the Jews have been in mortal danger."

"What does this have to do with us?" Jozef asked.

"We need you to take in the boy as your own," Herzog declared. Without waiting for a response, he stepped outside and brought Gideon in. Pointing to the stunned occupants, Herzog bent down and told Gideon, "These people are our friends. You're going to stay with them until we come back to pick you up."

Motioning for Paulina to take Gideon, Herzog whispered to Jozef, "I am making you, your wife, and brother-in-law fully responsible to us and the rest of the partisans for this boy's safety and well-being. If you take care of him through the rest of the war, you will be handsomely rewarded. If anything bad happens to this child, we will come here and burn all of you alive in this house."

Herzog never told them Gideon's name or that his father was one of Slovakia's most prominent rabbis. All they knew was that the boy was under the partisans' protection and that the peasants' lives depended on his safety. "There can be no excuses," Herzog stressed. "You must shelter him from any harm."

"We promise to take care of the child," said Jozef. "You have my word on it."

Just then Paulina noticed dried blood on the stocking of Gideon's right leg. She went over to him, rolled down the stocking, and exclaimed, "Oh, my God. You've been shot!"

She cleaned off the blood from the back of his leg, revealing flesh wounds from two machine-gun bullets. "He had been shot twice in the leg, but the bullets went through without shattering any bone or severing an artery."

"Didn't you feel any pain?" Jozef asked him.

The boy shrugged. "Maybe a little."

Up until then, Gideon had been so traumatized that he hadn't realized he had been shot. Because of the cold, the blood had clotted quickly, and the stocking had acted like a pressure bandage.

After treating the wound, Paulina fixed the partisans a hot meal, which they gladly ate. She also gave them fresh bread for their return trip. When the men said good-bye to Gideon, Herzog patted him on the head and said, "You will be safe here. Be a good boy."

Gideon nodded. Herzog then whispered to the couple, "Remember, if anything happens to this little boy, we will kill you."

Herzog had to talk tough to the peasants because he believed that only the fear of death would help secure the boy's life. Some peasants secretly worked for the Gestapo, so the threat of being burned alive was the best method to deal with those whose loyalty was unknown. Gideon had to be more precious to the three peasants than their own lives if the boy was to escape death at the hands of the enemy.

Jozef, a Polish-born cobbler, and Paulina, a native Slovakian, didn't need to be intimidated into caring for Gideon. They embraced the little boy as their own and told him to call them Uncle Jozef and Aunt Paulina. They were extremely kind to him and made sure he was fed, always sharing what little food they had.

Despite the fact that they were uneducated and lived a simple life, they were clever and smart in many ways. The first thing they did to protect him was to create a cover story and teach him to live as a Catholic.

"We're going to play a little game of pretend," Jozef told Gideon. "From now on, you have a new name—Jan Suchy. You are not Jewish but Catholic. And you are the son of Aunt Paulina's brother who was killed by the partisans."

"But the partisans are my friends," Gideon said.

"Yes, I know. But you must pretend they are not. You must make believe that your pretend father was killed by the partisans so that the Germans will think he was murdered for being on their side. That way they will have great sympathy for you."

To help create the cover, the couple taught him the Lord's Prayer. They knew that enemy soldiers sometimes would test a child to see if he really was Christian by demanding he recite the prayer. If he couldn't, that was proof enough for them that he was Jewish.

"This is an important game, Jan," Jozef said, using Gideon's new name. "Everyone's life depends on how good you are at playing it."

Gideon learned the prayer and adopted his fake identity. Although he was scared playing this strange pretend game, he realized that in war he must do things he didn't fully understand. It was, as his new "aunt" and "uncle" stressed, a matter of life and death.

Uncle Jozef and Aunt Paulina wouldn't let him talk about his real family for fear he would slip and say something to a soldier. Gideon accepted the sad truth that his mother and sister were dead, and he had no idea where his father was or even if he was alive. So the boy lived in the present, just hoping to make it through the day without being discovered.

"You need to fear all the soldiers," Jozef warned him. "The Wehrmacht—those are the regular German soldiers—only kill as ordered by their superiors. Be more scared of the men in black—the S.S. They are trained killers. But the ones you need to fear the most are the Ukrainian nationalists. They're the ones who wear white camouflage. They kill for fun."

Whenever Gideon and the other children saw the Ukrainians coming down the mountain toward the village, everyone scurried to his or her home. Nobody remained in the street, and every house was shuttered.

Several times a week, enemy soldiers would surround the hamlet and search one or more houses. One day, soldiers stormed the neighbor's home. Gideon and his new family sat on the floor of their own house, scared to death. From a few yards away, he heard the neighbors' screams as they were being beaten by the soldiers.

"The Germans must have found a Jew or partisan hiding in their home," Jozef said.

"But we've had partisans come here, too," Gideon whispered.

"Yes, I know."

After more screams and yelling from next door, Gideon heard shots. Then the soldiers left. Seconds later, the house burst into flames—with the neighbors inside.

Within days, the Wehrmacht conducted another house-to-house search for Jews and partisans. When they reached the Strycharczyk home, Gideon wasn't too worried because the partisans were always careful not to leave any trace of their visits. But in the attic, the soldiers found five rounds of ammunition accidentally left behind by several partisans who had spent the night. Jozef was arrested and taken away while several soldiers stood guard outside the house.

Seeing Paulina and her brother nervously pacing the floor, Gideon fretted. He knew that if Uncle Jozef was sent away or killed for collaborating with the partisans or for harboring a Jew, he and the others would likely be murdered.

Late in the day, Paulina let out a shout of joy. Jozef had returned unharmed. "All is well," he announced. "When I was arrested, I told the commander that the partisans had stayed with us. I said, 'Your soldiers aren't protecting us in Bully. At night, you leave and the partisans come down from the mountains and threaten us if we don't let them sleep in the attic, where it is warm. Then they steal our food and leave. What can we do? If you would stay here through the night and protect us, there would be no reason for the partisans to come into Bully anymore.' The commander believed me and let me go."

Jozef looked at Gideon and added, "The commander never questioned why we have a new member of the family."

"Thank goodness it was the Wehrmacht who arrested you," said Paulina. "If the Ukrainians had found those same bullets, they would not have listened to any explanation. They would have burned the house down with all of us in it."

Meanwhile, high in the mountains, Herzog and his men continued to fight for their lives. Whenever they met fellow Jews, they told them about Gideon and where he was staying. Herzog hoped that if Rabbi Frieder somehow survived the war, he would learn from others where to find his son.

In spring 1945, word reached the tiny hamlet that Slovakia had been liberated. Soon two men arrived at the Strycharczyk home and announced, "We've come to bring young Gideon back to his father." They presented the couple with a letter from Rabbi Frieder, thanking them for taking care of Gideon. He had traced his son's whereabouts through information planted by Herzog and the partisans.

In a tearful good-bye, Paulina hugged the boy and told him, "You don't have to pretend who you are anymore. You are once again Gideon Frieder."

=====

Of the 135,000 Jews who lived in Slovakia before the war, only about 25,000 survived. After liberation, the country became part of Czechoslovakia with a new government that executed many of Slovakia's top officials who had sided with the Nazis.

Gideon was reunited with his father, who married a woman whose husband had been killed in the war. Sadly, Rabbi Frieder died a year later during gall bladder surgery. He was only 35 years old.

Armed with fake identity cards, Gideon and his stepmother settled in Israel, where he grew up and became a specialist in the Ministry of Defense. With the help of his uncle, who was also a rabbi, the bodies of Gideon's mother, sister, and father were exhumed and properly reburied in Israel.

In 1975, Gideon immigrated to the United States, where he was a professor at the State University of New York at Buffalo. He eventually became the dean of the School of Engineering at George Washington University in Washington, D.C. Today he holds the A. James Clark Chair of Engineering and Applied Science at the university. He speaks about the Holocaust as a Survivor Volunteer at the United States Holocaust Memorial Museum.

Gideon, the father of three and grandfather of two, took his family back to Slovakia in 1999. At the site where his mother and sister were killed, they stacked stones as a memorial and said Kaddish (a prayer said by mourners over the death of a loved one).

They also met Anastazia Ivanicova, the daughter of Jozef and Paulina Strycharczyk, who was born a month after Gideon had been returned to his father. Recalling his emotional meeting with Anastazia, Gideon said, "She told me her parents always talked about me until their deaths in 1975. They said that if she should ever meet me, she should treat me as her brother because they intended to keep me. She told me, 'Before you leave, I want to give you my greatest treasure. I got it from my parents. They told me it was the most precious thing they owned. I want you to have it.' She gave me the note I had written to them in December 1945. I told her, 'No way will I take it from you.' I made a copy, and it's framed and hanging in my home. The note said, 'Dear Uncle, I thank you very much for everything, and I wish you and Aunt a pleasant holiday and happy New Year. Yours with thanks. Gideon.'"

Henry Herzog survived the war and lives in Florida. He wrote his memoir, And Heaven Shed No Tears, from which some material translated by Gideon was used in this story.

"I Defeated Them All . . . and I'm Still Alive!"

≡

Hanci Hollander

For four agonizing days, 14-year-old Hanci Hollander and her family rode in a tightly packed cattle car with barely any food or water. It was so crammed that her older brothers had to sleep standing up, leaning on one another's shoulders while she lay under their feet. The air was thick with the smell of sweat and a cloud of misery. So when the train carrying thousands of Jewish prisoners reached its destination, Hanci and everyone else were relieved.

If only they knew where they had arrived.

When the locked doors were thrown open, Hanci sucked in her first breath of fresh air—and nearly gagged from an overwhelming stench. Instantly, she felt the presence of evil. *I don't like what I see*, she thought. Her eyes studied the tall barbed-wire electrified fences, the rows of gray barracks, and the menacing guards waving their machine guns.

"Out! Out!" the guards shouted. Frightened and bewildered, Hanci and the others hustled past snarling, snapping German shepherds straining on leashes, ready to pounce and tear apart anyone on command.

Yelps and cries from prisoners who were whipped or beaten mingled with the voices of soldiers bellowing orders to form lines — one for females and one for males. Without a chance to say good-bye, Hanci and her younger sister and mother were separated from her father and two of her brothers.

The brutal troops marched the prisoners toward a handsome S.S. officer who wore a perfectly tailored, pressed uniform. In one of his white-gloved hands, he gripped a riding crop. Rather than strike the prisoners with it, he pointed it to the left or right, indicating which direction he wanted each Jew to go.

What Hanci and the others didn't know was that this elegant officer was selecting those for slave labor and those for the gas chambers. The man, who liked to whistle songs from his favorite operas while deciding who lived and who died, was the notorious Dr. Josef Mengele, otherwise known as the Angel of Death.

Hanci and the new arrivals were clueless about one other frightening reality: They had arrived at Auschwitz II–Birkenau, the nightmarish killing factory in southwestern Poland where thousands of Jews were being gassed and then cremated every day.

Growing up in Czechoslovakia, Zora "Hanci" Hollander lived with her parents and five siblings in a seven-room house on a farm stocked with horses, cows, chickens, and other animals in the town of Nagy Bereg, population 6,000. She loved school and dreamed of becoming a teacher when she grew up.

But in 1939, when she was nine, the region was taken over by a pro-Nazi, anti-Semitic Hungarian government. Her father, David, a successful farmer and store owner, lost control of everything he owned but his farm, store, and vineyards because of anti-Jewish laws. Hanci and her siblings attended Hungarian-speaking schools — and eventually were forced to sit in the back of the classroom because they were Jewish.

In spring 1944, the Hollanders celebrated Passover, marking the liberation of the Jews from slavery in Egypt more than 3,000 years before. On the final day of the holiday, the town's mayor — a Christian friend of David's — came at night and warned, "The Germans are going to take you and your whole family away. In fact, they're rounding up all the Jews in town early in the morning and shipping them to the ghetto in Beregszász. From there, who knows? I'm so sorry, David. There's no escape. The Germans have sealed off the town. I must go. If they see me here, they might deport me, too."

Because radios had been confiscated and newspapers were censored, people in the region didn't know the Nazis were exterminating Jews.

When the mayor left, David called the family together and broke the news of their deportation. "They are taking us from the house where you were all born and the land that has belonged to our family for generations," he said. "We must prepare." Because homes didn't have phones, Hanci's brothers Miksa, 21, Sanyi, 19, and Viktor, 17, ran out to warn relatives and Jewish friends. Then they helped their father hide the family valuables, burying the silverware and candelabra in the dirt floor in the utility room. All the jewelry was placed in a metal box and concealed under the hardwood floorboards of a back bedroom. "These valuables could always be sold when we return or if we move to another country after the war is over," Hanci's mother, Helen, explained.

Hanci, her sister, Annuska, 12, and their brothers packed their good clothes and an extra pair of shoes. After the children went to bed, Helen began making bread for the trip. Hanci didn't sleep much that night, fretting over what to do with her pet cat, Juci, and what the new day would bring.

At 5 A.M., German soldiers pounded on the door and announced, "You have thirty minutes to leave and go to City Hall!"

Hanci nervously braided her pigtails, put on a nice dress, and stepped into the new shoes that she had received for

Passover. Then she and her siblings each took a suitcase or a woven bag and loaded it onto their horse-drawn wagon.

When the time came to leave, Hanci, holding Juci in her arms, went into the barn, where she found her father gently brushing the horses and cows. He gave each a loving hug. "The soldiers are waiting for you, Father," she said.

"I'll be there in a minute, honey," he replied, wiping away his tears. It was the first time Hanci had seen him cry since her eldest brother, Jozsi, was killed in an accident.

Hanci shed her own tears moments later when she gave Juci to her neighbor, Irma Neni, who promised to take care of the cat until the Hollanders returned home.

David reluctantly turned over the keys to the Hungarian police and the German S.S. soldiers. They put a lock on the front door, dripped hot wax onto the lock, and imprinted it with the Nazi swastika. As the family left, Hanci smelled the bread that was still baking in the oven.

At City Hall, the Hollanders and all the other Jews in Nagy Bereg were put into trucks and driven to the nearby city of Beregszász. For the next four weeks, the family lived with thousands of other deported Jews in a filthy, overcrowded ghetto on the grounds of a brick factory. The place brought back bad memories for Hanci because it was where Jozsi had died in an accident in 1941. Days after the family arrived, Miksa was drafted by the Hungarian army.

A month later, the remaining Hollanders found themselves in Auschwitz II–Birkenau facing Dr. Mengele. He sent healthy men who looked between 16 and 50 years old—including Hanci's father, David, and brothers Sanyi and Viktor—one direction; healthy women—including Hanci and her mother—another way; and the old, disabled, ill, and most children in a third direction. Annuska was ordered to go with the last group.

"Don't worry about Annuska," Helen told Hanci. "She is with the older people, so they will look after her. Our group is probably the workforce."

A short while later, as the women were being led to a barrack, Hanci noticed a horse-drawn wagon filled with the new arrivals' luggage, baskets, and bundles. Sitting in the back of the wagon was Annuska, dangling her legs. When she spotted Hanci, she jumped off and joined them.

"What is wrong with you, Annuska?" her mother scolded. "You should have stayed with the older people."

"I wanted to be with you and Hanci because a soldier was being mean to me," she countered. "He gave me a good whack with his rifle for no reason. When I saw a wagon going in your direction, I thought, *What can they do to me? Give me another whack?* I hopped onto the back and kept looking for you and Hanci. I was lucky to find you."

"Not so lucky," said Helen. "Now you'll have to work hard and for long hours. You are so young and won't be able to keep up with us."

"I'll be a good worker," Annuska pledged. "You'll see."

The women were ushered into a building where their earrings were either cut off or ripped off their ears. Then their heads were shaved. When a guard snipped off Hanci's two long braids and tossed them into a growing pile of hair, the teenager was mortified. She was even more humiliated when the rest of her hair ended up on the floor after being shaved off. Hanci, who was always proud of her thick, auburn hair, had never felt uglier—a feeling made worse when guards called the women *Untermenschen*, German for "subhumans."

Then came the next phase of dehumanization: Each prisoner selected for slave labor was branded with a number. As far as the Germans were concerned, Hanci no longer had a name at Auschwitz II–Birkenau. From now on, she was number A-6374. Her mother was A-6372 and Annuska was A-6373. The numbers were tattooed in dark blue ink on their lower left arm.

Hanci and the others were put in a women's barrack that housed about 1,000 sullen, pale-skinned prisoners who had been slave laborers for months. Seeing how depressed they looked, Hanci convinced 10 teenage girls who had arrived with her to sing in an effort to cheer up everyone.

Most of the inmates stared blankly at the singing girls. Perplexed by the lack of any appreciation from the women, Hanci pressed on with her attempt to brighten their day. She and the girls composed a song: "Rows of barracks in a camp somewhere in the world, Jews line up to be counted with tears in their eyes. Wretched, cold, soaking wet, the rain is pouring down, they must line up in spite of the weather. Be strong and brave, heroic Jewish worker. The day of freedom will come soon—the great day, the day of reckoning when Jewish suffering will end forever. We will be strong and live to do our best to overcome this. The time will come when we will return to our beautiful homes and into the arms of our loved ones. This is our song and it will be until we die, and our Jewish heritage we will never deny."

Although she was puzzled that the prisoners still weren't smiling, Hanci encouraged her friends to take turns singing solo. One girl stood on a stool and belted out a tune when unexpectedly the female barrack supervisor rushed up and slapped her hard in the face, knocking her to the floor.

"Where do you think you are?" the woman hissed at the stunned girl. "In a hotel? On vacation? This isn't a resort. It's a *death* camp!" Pointing out the window to several buildings in the distance, she said, "Do you see those smokestacks? That's where your loved ones have been gassed and burned. The smoke you see is from their burning bodies!"

What? Is she crazy? Hanci thought. *How could that be? She must be trying to scare us, that's all. The Germans wouldn't do this to us. How cruel she is to say such horrible things.*

Later that night, Hanci approached an inmate who had been at Auschwitz II–Birkenau for several months and asked, "That mean woman was trying to scare us, right?"

"Yes, but she was also telling the truth," the prisoner replied. "This really is a death camp. They really are exterminating the Jews."

"I don't believe you," Hanci declared, and stormed off. *She's saying that because she and the others are jealous of us,* Hanci thought. *We still look better than they do even though we haven't had a bath in over a month.*

Seeking reassurance, Hanci talked to other prisoners and heard the same story. "We're trying to break the truth gently to you," said one of them. "The officer who separated everyone into three lines when you arrived is Dr. Josef Mengele. He sends the able-bodied men in one direction for slave labor and does the same for the women who can work."

"And the third group?"

The woman shook her head. "They all die in the gas chambers within ninety minutes of arriving here, and their bodies are burned."

Hanci shuddered as she grasped the ghastly horror, especially when she realized how close her sister came to death. *Oh, my God!* Hanci thought. *Annuska saved herself by jumping onto that wagon. If she hadn't done that, she would be dead!*

Hanci and the girls never sang in the barrack again.

Every morning before sunup the whistle blew, and she and the prisoners in her barrack bailed out of their overcrowded bunks. They rushed through the narrow door only to have guards on each side whip them. She avoided being among the last ones out because the guards lashed them with relish. By the end of the first month at Auschwitz II–Birkenau, Hanci had nasty slash marks on her limbs.

Lining up outside, the prisoners stood at *Appell* and started counting and recounting, sometimes for hours. Periodically, the guards would select groups of inmates and take them away, never to return. Hanci knew where they were going—directly to the gas chambers. Life and death here was all a matter of luck. It didn't matter where you stood at *Appell*; your chances of getting picked were the same. The guards sometimes chose prisoners from one end of the row, sometimes from the other end, and sometimes from the middle. Hanci never felt safe anywhere.

The worst moments were Dr. Mengele's "special selections." Women had to remove their clothes while he looked them over to see if they were still healthy enough to work. He would move his little baton in a circular motion to indicate to the petrified prisoner to turn around so that he could inspect her backside. Then, with a tap of his baton, he would pick out the ones for the gas chamber. For Hanci, the crushing anxiety that he would select her mother or sister—or herself—nearly squeezed the air out of her lungs. While they stood in line waiting for his life-or-death decisions, many prisoners crumbled under the tension and fainted. They were dragged away and gassed.

The prisoners never got enough to eat, only a piece of bread in the morning and evening. Hanci used to save her bread to eat later, but after having it stolen a few times, Helen advised her, "Eat it when you get it. At least you know it's in your stomach."

At night, when Hanci and the other inmates crammed into their bunks, they took turns picking the lice off one another's bodies. "The Germans won't let us take a bath or clean ourselves," she complained to her mother. "They're trying to take away our humanity."

"We must stay strong," Helen said. "Our humanity is all we have left."

The inmates marched to work, going through the gates of several sets of electrified wire fences before reaching the forested area that shaded the gas chambers, which were more than a mile from the main camp. Along the way, Hanci sometimes saw bodies hanging limp on the fences—prisoners who chose electrocution over life.

Hanci and her sister and mother were assigned to the *Kanada* work detail behind Gas Chamber and Crematorium IV, where every day she glimpsed long columns of people walking into the structure but never coming out. The smoke billowing from the chimneys of the crematoriums created such a sickening stench that Hanci threw up for days. But eventually, the reeking odor no longer bothered her. She had lost her sense of smell.

The Hollanders worked in one of the 30 warehouses filled with the possessions of the new arrivals. In grueling 12-hour shifts with little food or water, the girls sorted through ceiling-high heaps of shoes, clothing, glasses, dentures, luggage, wedding bands, jewelry, and other belongings. Their job was to find anything of value—such as money or diamonds that had been sewn into cuffs, collars, and hems—and turn the booty over to the S.S. Whenever the girls found stale bread or a cookie in a pocket, they ate it when the guards weren't looking.

One day while sorting through the garments, Hanci came across a pile of clothes that she instantly recognized.

This is Aunt Piroska's dress! And here is Uncle Farkas's suit! This is what they were wearing when I last saw them. She felt sick to her stomach. Her hands trembled as she held some of their little children's clothes, all neatly folded. Thinking of her cousins, she thought, *I hope they didn't know they were going to their deaths.*

To maintain her sense of humanity, Hanci created stories in her mind about the people whose clothes she handled. Caressing a pair of soccer shoes, she envisioned that they belonged to a strapping young lad who had kicked the game-winning goal. A flowered dress conjured up an image of a young woman strolling through a garden arm in arm with her boyfriend. Hanci's stories gave her confirmation that the clothes were once worn by good, decent people just like her.

Too often, though, her imagination was jarred back to reality by a scream or a cry from a fellow worker who grumbled, cursed, or mouthed off to a guard and felt the crack of a whip or the butt of a gun. *Don't talk back*, Hanci reminded herself. *Just do as you're told and maybe you'll survive.*

One of the guards, a Hungarian who watched over the *Kanada* detail, took a casual interest in the Hollanders. He occasionally whispered a friendly greeting to them even though prisoners and guards weren't supposed to chat with one another. One time, he took out his wallet and, when the other guards weren't looking, showed the Hollanders a photo of a girl about eight years old. "This is my granddaughter back in Hungary," he told them, flashing a proud smile. "Someday I hope to see her again." Then, glancing over his shoulder to make sure no one else could hear him, he added grimly, "I'm not here in Auschwitz by choice."

A few weeks later, while sorting through the clothes, Helen found some food, wrapped it in cloth, and weighed it down with pebbles. Heading back to the barrack after their shift, Hanci saw her mother throw the food over the electric wire fence into an area where others from their hometown were being held. To Hanci's alarm, a guard saw Helen toss the food, so he grabbed her by the neck and rushed her off to the commandant's office. "Mother is going to be beaten or killed!" Hanci cried to Annuska.

After a tense 30 minutes, Helen returned to the barrack with a half smile on her face. "I'm fine," she told her worried daughters. Referring to an inmate who was in charge of a prisoner work detail, she explained, "The *kapo* went with me and told the commandant, 'She is the mother of the best little worker I have. If the mother dies, so will the daughter.' He was talking about you, Annuska. You work harder than anyone, just like you promised you would."

"Mother, I hope you won't ever do anything that foolish again," Hanci said.

"Honey," Helen replied, "you have to do some good whenever and wherever you can—even here."

The girl worried constantly about her mother's health. Everyone was sick and weak from exhaustion and hunger, but Helen was getting frail. One time when the prisoners had to stand at *Appell* for hours in the broiling summer sun,

Helen, who had nothing to cover her head, fainted. "If the guards see her, they'll take her straight to the gas chambers," Hanci told Annuska. She and her sister lifted their mother while guards walked up and down each row, counting. "Open your eyes, Mother, open your eyes!" Hanci pleaded. While her daughters held her from behind, Helen fluttered her eyes just as the guards strode past and counted her.

Such close calls happened more than once. *It could be our turn to die anytime, any minute, any hour, any day, any night,* Hanci thought. *When will it come? Who will die first? How will it happen? Will we collapse and die before we are picked out in a selection?*

In Auschwitz II–Birkenau, there was no time to brood. Hanci had to muster all her strength so that she could finish her work shift and hope to see the sun rise the next day.

She knew better than to think of escape. "They purposely keep us on a low-calorie diet so that we won't have the strength to run away," she told Annuska. "And even if you do escape, not having any hair makes it obvious to anyone on the outside that you are an escapee. And where would you run to, anyway? Every area is surrounded by tall electric-wire fences. There's no way to escape, nowhere to run."

Toward the end of 1944, Dr. Mengele called for another of his dreaded special selections. It was the sixth one that the Hollanders had faced. So far, they had beaten the odds. *How many times can we survive without one of us being picked?* Hanci wondered. She worried that he would think 48-year-old Helen was too old or that 12-year-old Annuska was too young, not to mention that Hanci herself was only 14 — two years younger than the typical cutoff age for slave laborers.

Everyone lined up, and despite the snow on the ground and the cold air, they were forced to take off their clothes. Then the Angel of Death slowly walked up and down the rows. Hanci held her breath. *Please don't take Mother or Annuska.* Mengele strolled over to Hanci and indicated with his baton for her to turn around. Like many of her fellow prisoners, Hanci was nothing but bones. *He's looking me over. Stand up straight. Look alert. Oh, I'm so scared I think I'm going to faint.*

Pointing to those he had already selected, he ordered Hanci to join them. Her mind reeled in terror, and her legs nearly buckled. *I've been given a death sentence!* As she shuffled off, she glanced back and saw the horror on her mother's face. *Poor Mother. She'll take my death so hard that she'll give up and die herself. And then Annuska will be left alone.*

"Good-bye, Mother," Hanci blurted.

Helen burst into tears. So did Annuska.

"Mother, don't cry. I'll see you again. Maybe not here but in heaven."

Not allowed to put on their clothes, Hanci and the 30 other selected prisoners were taken to a special barrack. Later that night, the doomed — many of them weeping — were loaded aboard a truck. The driver walked to the back of the vehicle to close the canvas drapes, but first he peered inside at the condemned. Hanci recognized him.

He was the friendly Hungarian guard who watched over the *Kanada* work group.

When he spotted Hanci, he looked stunned. "You, too?" he said to her.

Hanci nodded, acknowledging her fate.

Addressing all the prisoners in the truck, he whispered, "You know that I'm taking you to the gas chamber. But whoever wants to jump off on the way, go ahead and do it. All I ask is that if they find you, do not give me away. I might be able to save other lives. If you do give me away, both you and I will be killed." He closed the canvas drapes, and the truck drove off.

The vehicle passed through several gates and crossed into another camp section before entering the enclosed forested area of the gas chambers.

Fighting off panic, Hanci told herself, *I have to save my life. If I stay on this truck, I'll be killed. If I jump, I might be found and then shot. At least I won't be gassed. But I want to live. Jumping out now is my only chance to live and see Mother again.*

"I'm going to jump out," she whispered to the others. "Who will come with me?"

Nobody responded. She understood. Most had lost their entire families and didn't have anyone or anything to live for, so they had given up. Others knew there was no way anyone could escape from here. "Our time has come," someone said wearily.

But Hanci didn't feel that way. She was young and foolish, and willing to take any chance that came her way.

She had nothing to lose. "Well, good-bye," she told them. Then she leaped off the back of the slow-moving truck and landed in the snow-packed road. She rolled down an embankment into a narrow ditch. Caked with snow and ice, Hanci crawled into a culvert and curled up in a ball. She had no idea what to do next. She had escaped, although she was still within the compound. Deciding to stay put, the girl wondered how long it would take before someone realized she was missing.

Fifteen minutes after she jumped, Hanci heard the wail of sirens alerting guards of an escape attempt. *They're looking for me now, and they're bringing their dogs.* She scrunched farther into the culvert. *I wonder if the dogs will pick up my scent in this cold.*

Soon she heard the voices of the S.S. and the crunch of boots in the snow. The footsteps and barking grew louder. *They're getting closer. Is this the end for me?* She was too scared to move a muscle. Minutes ticked off and then . . . *They passed by me. They didn't find me!*

Despite being naked in the dead of winter, she didn't feel cold. Fear of being discovered had trumped any sensation of feeling chilled to the bone. As the hours wore on, she felt a new sensation—one of triumph. *I've defeated them all and I'm still alive, at least for another day!*

Still afraid that guards were quietly nearby, Hanci remained in the culvert until the middle of the following night. About 24 hours after she had been selected for death, Hanci began thinking about her next move. *I can't stay here much longer. I'd better do something, because I'll either starve to death or freeze to death. I must leave my hiding place and figure out exactly where I am.*

She emerged from the culvert and scrambled up to the road. But in the darkness, she became confused. She knew she was still inside the prison complex behind several electrified fences, and breaching them would be nearly impossible. Her top priority was surviving—and that meant finding clothes and food.

In the distance, Hanci saw a tiny light coming from the window of a building. Every barrack in the sprawling camp had blackout shades or shutters, but this particular window leaked light. To Hanci, it looked like a little star, so she decided to follow it, not knowing where it would lead her.

Ignoring the frigid air that had sucked all the warmth out of her bare body, she trudged through the frosty silent night until she reached the barrack. The light had been turned off. *It could be a women's barrack. But maybe it's a men's barrack. Or what if it's S.S. headquarters? I can't stay out here much longer or I'll die. I've got to go inside and take the risk.*

Fortunately, there was no guard on duty. Hanci tiptoed into the pitch-black barrack and, by feeling around, discovered it was filled with bunks. Judging from the snorts and snoring, she knew it was a prisoners' barrack. *Is it a men's or a women's? There's only one way to find out.* She climbed up to the third tier of a bunk where an inmate was sleeping in a large man's coat. Feeling Hanci's ice-cold body, the prisoner screamed. It was a woman. Cupping her hand over her mouth, Hanci pleaded, "Shush, don't give me away. I was on my way to the gas chamber and I escaped. Please let me stay here. I have no clothes or shoes. I have nowhere to go."

"You poor dear," the woman said. Taking off her overcoat, she tenderly wrapped it around Hanci. "Stay here for the night."

Through chattering teeth, the shivering girl explained what had happened to her. "I want to get back to my mother and sister."

"I'm not sure that's possible, dear. You see, all of us were transferred here earlier in the day. We're being transported to another camp in the morning."

At daybreak, the barefoot Hanci, clutching the overcoat, lined up with the others from the barrack for *Appell*. Her bunkmate was wearing a coat taken off an inmate who had died during the night. Luckily, the guards were in too much of a hurry to get an accurate count. Everyone in the barrack was then shoved onto cattle cars and shipped out.

As the train left Auschwitz II–Birkenau, Hanci felt torn. She was relieved to depart the death camp that had been her prison for seven months, but she was sad to leave her mother and sister behind. *Will we ever be together again?*

The train rolled through the countryside for several days while Hanci, who hadn't eaten or drunk anything since her escape, grew extremely weak and sick. But others were in worse shape and fell dead by the hour. Despite her condition, she had the presence of mind to take wooden shoes off a corpse and put them on her frozen feet.

The effects of hunger made Hanci woozy. Her empty stomach ached, and her parched tongue stuck to the roof of her mouth. Her joints stiffened and her rail-thin limbs jerked. She felt dazed and almost didn't care anymore whether she lived or died. *I feel so helpless. I'm going to topple over any minute and never get up. It's very easy to give up.* But then she waged a mental battle with herself. *No, I can't. I have to keep going until the end. I must live. I must do it for Mother. I must see her again.*

After several agonizing days and nights in cattle cars, the prisoners arrived at Bergen-Belsen concentration camp, where Hanci turned 15 — a birthday that came and went unobserved. Then she was transported from one camp to another, forced to work as a slave laborer for the Nazis. Under armed guard, she toiled on an assembly line for 12 hours a day making gas masks in Hannover. In the cities of Hamburg and Braunschweig, she helped clear the streets of debris from buildings that the Allies had bombed.

In one of the camps, the prisoners' hands were inspected. Those like Hanci who had small hands were shipped to Beendorf, Germany. There, they worked 1,200 feet underground in a salt mine converted into a secret factory that manufactured parts for the deadly V1 and V2 missiles that were wreaking havoc on Great Britain. The small-handed inmates were forced to make delicate parts for the rockets.

Hanci, who operated a machine, thought about committing sabotage but decided against it. The slightest infraction was punishable by a bullet in the head. Besides, her work was inspected seconds after she finished each part.

Because she was suffering from severe malnutrition, it was hard for Hanci to concentrate. She also was in pain because the salt dust kicked up by the inmates when they marched into the converted mine stung the open sores on her right leg. Nevertheless, she felt lucky because she worked under the eyes of a kind civilian trainer who took pity on her. He left her a portion of his lunch each day—a thoughtful gesture that gave Hanci strength to carry on.

Unexpectedly, Hanci and the others were moved out of Beendorf and sent to the all-women Ravensbrück concentration camp—her seventh camp.

Soon, though, they were shipped in locked boxcars toward an unknown destination. Hanci wondered if the Germans were losing the war because the soldiers seemed much more nervous, frustrated, and cruel. For three days, the train traveled seemingly without direction throughout northern Germany, stopping frequently.

Lacking food and water, the weary and weak began dying in great numbers. It was all Hanci could do to stay alive, reminding herself, *I must live if I ever want to see Mother and Annuska*. She refused to believe they were dead.

In the boxcar, Hanci noticed a sick, moaning woman who reminded her of her mother. "Are you in pain?" Hanci asked. The woman opened her coat, revealing a shrunken body covered with blisters. "You look like you are hurting all over," Hanci said. "Let me help you to a corner, and I'll stand over you to make sure no one falls on you."

"You're so kind," the woman said. "You look so weak and sick yourself. Why would you help me?

"You remind me of my mother. I last saw her in Auschwitz."

"I lost many relatives there."

"I'll be your daughter, and you can be my mother until this war is over."

Seeing that Hanci was wearing wooden shoes, the woman pointed to her own nice leather shoes and said, "When I die you can have them."

"No, you'll need them when you greet your family after the war."

Minutes later, the woman closed her eyes and took her final breath. Hanci wept for her.

Soon the train stopped in the middle of nowhere, and Hanci could hear German soldiers milling about outside. Prisoners whose ears were pressed against the walls of the boxcar uttered cries of alarm. "They're planning to kill us!" one of them shouted. "They're going to line us up and machine-gun us!"

Hanci was too hungry and thirsty and sick and tired to feel much fear. *I guess this is really it. At least death will end my misery.* But then, thinking about her mother and sister, Hanci discovered that her will to live hadn't totally withered. *There must be a way.*

The doors opened and the guards shouted, "Throw out all the dead and the sick right now!"

About half the prisoners in the boxcars were dead. Hanci gently picked up her friend's body and lowered it to the ground, saying, "Good-bye, my friend. I'll see you in heaven." Hanci chose not to take the woman's shoes.

The inmates removed the corpses, but they refused to toss out the sick. "The Germans are going to kill us whether we do what they say or not, so let the sick stay here and come what may," a prisoner said.

When the bodies were stacked, the survivors were ordered out of the boxcars and told to line up. Hanci looked around. The train had stopped in the middle of a vast meadow. *It's a perfect place to execute us,* she thought. *There's no one else around.*

"Move! Move!" the guards shouted. "Walk in a straight line!"

Thousands upon thousands of ragged, scrawny women staggered away from the train and toward the killing field. But then they were told to stop. Up ahead, Hanci noticed the officers in charge were holding a meeting. Soon several trucks appeared. *What is going on?* she wondered.

Hours passed, and the German soldiers began acting strangely. Some seemed pleased and others appeared angry or confused. To the utter disbelief of the prisoners, the soldiers began doling out a handful of sugar and a handful of uncooked macaroni to each woman.

When it was Hanci's turn in line, she could barely stand. The feeble girl held out the front of her dress to collect her allotment of macaroni and sugar. But when she looked down, she became distraught. Because of the mental fog she had been in, she wasn't aware until that moment that her dress was full of holes. Everything she had received had spilled onto the grass. *No, this can't be happening to me!* She bent down to pick up the macaroni.

Out of sheer cruelty, a guard clubbed her on the head with his rifle. Just as the pain began to register in her brain, he struck her again . . . and everything went black.

Much later, when Hanci woke up, she was slumped over in the seat of a passenger train that was chugging through the countryside. "Where am I? What happened?" the groggy girl asked the woman next to her.

"We are free! We are in Denmark."

I must be hallucinating, Hanci thought. Throughout her imprisonment, she heard many stories that weren't true, tales that fellow inmates invented to keep hope alive. *She's either telling stories or I'm dreaming.* Hanci passed out again. When she regained consciousness, she asked her companion, "Is it true? Are we really free, or is it a dream?"

"It's a dream come true."

"What happened to me? The last thing I remember was getting beaten."

"The Germans left you to die, but we wouldn't, so we carried you back to the boxcar. A guard asked us, 'Why are you dragging a dead person?' And I said, 'She's not dead. She just fainted.'"

"Thank you. It's comforting to know there are prisoners still capable of human feelings and compassion. You and the others could hardly walk, yet you still did this for me. I would have died there if you hadn't picked me up."

"You would have done the same for us. I saw how you helped the woman with all the blisters."

"I thought we were going to be executed."

"We all did. And we would have been had it not been for the Swedish Red Cross."

Count Folke Bernadotte of Sweden—a member of the Swedish royal family, a diplomat, and leader of the Swedish Red Cross—had negotiated with powerful Nazi official Heinrich Himmler for the release of thousands of Scandinavian prisoners and Jews from several concentration camps, including Ravensbrück. The deal was reached shortly before the prisoners on the train were to be executed.

Now, as the train neared the Danish capital, Copenhagen, Hanci overheard a German soldier telling several former prisoners, "You are lucky. You are free. I have to go back to Germany and face the music because the war is ending."

At first, Hanci wondered why the freed prisoners on the train weren't in a more festive mood. Most everyone seemed enveloped in a cloud of sorrow. Then she understood why:

We're all hungry and sick and weak. We try to laugh and smile, but maybe we forgot how.

As the train arrived in Copenhagen, she heard church bells ringing and saw Danes by the thousands waving their country's flag and shouting "Welcome!" Tears trickled down Hanci's face, and a smile — a big smile — spread across her face. And it felt so good.

═══

During World War II, the Nazis deported 437,000 Czechoslovakian and Hungarian Jews to death camps. Hanci was one of only 20,000 of them who survived.

She was taken to Landskrona, Sweden, where she was put in quarantine and then nursed back to health by a kindhearted family, Erik and Lilly Berglund and their 14-year-old daughter, Gullan. During that time, Hanci wrote many letters home, hoping to learn about her family. For months, she never received a reply, because the Soviet Union had taken control of Hungary and had blocked virtually all communication with those trapped behind the Iron Curtain. But she never gave up believing that her family had survived.

Finally, months after the war, she received a letter from her mother with the incredible family news that everyone but Hanci's brother Viktor had survived and was back home. Tragically, Viktor had been beaten to death by a German guard just three days before Auschwitz II–Birkenau was liberated.

The letter said that after liberation, radio announcements were broadcast from Sweden throughout Europe listing names of Holocaust survivors. Family friends rushed to the Hollanders' home, saying, "We heard Hanci's name over the radio! She's recovering in Sweden!" But Helen refused to believe it, claiming, "Nobody who went to the gas chamber ever came out alive." Hanci's brother Miksa then went to Budapest and returned home with an official list of Hungarian survivors in Sweden that included Hanci's name. But Helen still wouldn't allow herself the joy of knowing that her daughter was alive. Not until all of Hanci's six letters arrived at the same time did Helen finally believe it.

In subsequent letters, Hanci learned that when the family was deported the house, furniture, animals, and farm equipment had been auctioned off. A new family lived in the house during the war but fled when the Russians liberated the area. When the Hollanders returned home, they found their house had been stripped of everything. The buried silverware was gone, but the jewelry hidden under the floor was recovered.

In answer to Hanci's question about the friendly guard at the Kanada work detail, Annuska replied that the guard was never seen again after the night that Hanci fled. No one knows if he was shot or transferred to the Russian front because of her escape.

In 1947, Hanci was given an opportunity to live with relatives in the United States. However, she had yet to *see her parents or siblings since escaping Auschwitz II–Birkenau. She yearned to be with them, but it would mean living under communist control behind the Iron Curtain. In a letter, she asked her mother, "What should I do with my life?" Helen wrote back, "As much as we'd love for you to come home, Father and I think you would have a better life in America."*

Saying good-bye to her adopted Swedish family, Hanci immigrated to Kansas City, Missouri, where, at the urging of her relatives, she Americanized her name, changing it to Gloria. In 1948, her mother died from complications of illnesses she had contracted in Auschwitz II–Birkenau.

Gloria married a young attorney, Karl Lyon, and moved to San Francisco, where she raised a family and worked for 20 years as a research analyst for two different financial institutions. Since 1980, she has owned and operated a bed-and-breakfast inn. The couple has two children, nine grandchildren, and two great-grandchildren. Over the years, Gloria and Karl brought all of her family out of the Soviet Union to the United States.

Gloria—who underwent 15 operations on her legs, hips, and back from the effects of malnutrition she suffered during the Holocaust—never spoke publicly about her childhood experience until she saw the cover of a vile brochure. It showed a black swastika over the Star of David and was titled "A Zionist Hoax: The Holocaust Never Happened."

At that moment in 1977, Gloria Lyon knew that she had an obligation to speak out. Since then she has made it her mission to educate young people about the Holocaust. "This is not just a Jewish story," she says. "It's a human story. If people don't know the truth about the Holocaust, then it could happen again to anybody, anywhere, at any time to any race or any color."

Although a doctor offered to remove her tattooed concentration-camp number, Gloria chose to keep it as a reminder of her survival. She's writing an auto-biography called Mommy, What's That Number on Your Arm? As part of a documentary film (available on DVD) about her suffering, called When I Was 14: A Survivor Remembers, Gloria and Karl went back to Europe to retrace her steps during the Holocaust. Her trip included a tour of Auschwitz II–Birkenau, which has been turned into a museum. After her emotional return to the notorious death camp, Gloria discovered something she hadn't experienced in nearly half a century: She regained her sense of smell.

About the Author

Allan Zullo is the author of nearly 100 nonfiction books on subjects ranging from sports and the supernatural to history and animals.

He has introduced Scholastic readers to the Ten True Tales series, gripping stories of extraordinary persons — many of them young people — who have met the challenges of dangerous, sometimes life-threatening, situations. Among the books in the series are *World War II Heroes* and *War Heroes: Voices from Iraq*. In addition, he has authored two other books about the real-life experiences of kids during the Holocaust: *Survivors: True Stories of Children in the Holocaust* and *Heroes of the Holocaust: True Stories of Rescues by Teens*.

Allan, the grandfather of four and the father of two grown daughters, lives with his wife, Kathryn, on the side of a mountain near Asheville, North Carolina.

To learn more about the author, visit his Web site at www.allanzullo.com.